Portion of a Cabinet,
executed from a Design by Charles L. Eastlake.

HINTS ON
HOUSEHOLD TASTE

THE CLASSIC HANDBOOK OF
VICTORIAN INTERIOR DECORATION

BY CHARLES L. EASTLAKE

⸺◆◆◆⸺

WITH A NEW INTRODUCTION BY
JOHN GLOAG

DOVER PUBLICATIONS, INC.
NEW YORK

Note on the cover photograph. The ebony library of *Glenview*, the John Bond Trevor Mansion at Yonkers, New York, accurately reflects the Eastlake style of interior decoration. Particularly noteworthy are the woodwork, stenciling, tiling and built-ins, all original to the mansion, which was built in 1876. Photograph by Scott Bowron courtesy of the Hudson River Museum, Yonkers, New York.

Published in Canada by General Publishing Company, Ltd., 30 Lesmill Road, Don Mills, Toronto, Ontario.
Published in the United Kingdom by Constable and Company, Ltd.

This Dover edition, first published in 1986, is an unabridged republication of the 1969 Dover edition of *Hints on Household Taste in Furniture, Upholstery and Other Details,* a republication of the 1878 fourth (revised) edition published by Longmans, Green and Company, London. For the 1969 Dover edition, an Introduction was prepared specially by John Gloag.
The original nine color plates from the 1878 edition are represented by black-and-white reproductions.

Manufactured in the United States of America
Dover Publications, Inc., 31 East 2nd Street, Mineola, N.Y. 11501

Library of Congress Cataloging-in-Publication Data

Eastlake, Charles L. (Charles Locke), 1836–1906.
Hints on household taste.

Reprint. Originally published: Hints on household taste in furniture, upholstery, and other details. 4th ed. London : Longmans, Green, 1878.
Includes index.
1. Interior decoration—History—19th century. 2. Decoration and ornament—Victorian style. I. Title.
NK1968.E3   1986   747.22   85-20723
ISBN 0-486-25046-6

INTRODUCTION
TO THE DOVER EDITION

N 1864 the March issue of *The Cornhill Magazine* included an essay on "The Fashion of Furniture," which expressed some refreshingly critical views.* Like most contributions to magazines in the early and mid-nineteenth century it was unsigned, but the editor of *The Queen*, attracted by the anonymous writer's originality, discovered that he was a young man of twenty-eight named Charles Locke Eastlake, and invited him to expand the subject in a series of articles. The first of these articles appeared in *The Queen* on June 24, 1865,† and the series, entitled "Hints on Household Taste," continued until late the following year. The author signed himself "Jack Easel," a pseudonym he revived thirty years later when he published his last book.

The articles were not illustrated, and Eastlake conceived the idea of recasting them, together with others he had contributed to the *London Review*, so they could appear in

* Vol. IX, No 51, pages 337–349.
† Vol. XXXVII, No. 965, pages 411–412.

book form with his own drawings. The book was accepted and published in 1868 by Longmans, Green and Company; the title used for *The Queen* articles was adopted and a subtitle added, so it became: *Hints on Household Taste, in Furniture, Upholstery and Other Details*; and in the preface the author stated that his object was "to suggest some fixed principles of taste for the popular guidance of those who are not accustomed to hear such principles defined."

Hints was a seductive word for wooing the book market; contemporary magazines were full of hints about social etiquette, polite recreations, the practice of home-crafts, appreciation of the arts, indeed everything that ministered to the Victorians' passion for self-improvement and dispelled their dread of idleness; morever *hints* implied that taste in household furnishing could be acquired painlessly, without arduous study though with confidence, for the author's professional standing guaranteed his authority. On the title page a small line of type below his name notified his fellowship of the Royal Institute of British Architects; and despite the intermittent thundering of Ruskin against architects and all their works, a general belief in the sanctity of professional qualifications remained unshaken. Eastlake's were indisputable: when his book first appeared he had for two years been Secretary of the R.I.B.A., and his family connections with the fine arts were impressive.

Charles Locke Eastlake was born at Plymouth, Devonshire, on March 11, 1836, the fourth son of George Eastlake, an Admiralty law agent and deputy judge advocate of the Fleet. He was named after his uncle, Sir Charles Lock Eastlake (who spelt his second name without the final e), a diligent but uninspired painter, who was knighted after his election as President of the Royal Academy in 1850. This mildly distinguished artist undoubtedly influenced and certainly assisted his nephew's early career.

Eastlake went to Westminster School, became a Queen's scholar in 1846, and after completing his education developed a respectable talent for drawing and painting in watercolours. He entered the Royal Academy schools, and an early interest in architecture was stimulated by the award of a silver medal for architectural drawings in 1854, and by the acceptance of two designs for exhibition at the Academy in 1855 and 1856. Meanwhile he was articled to an accomplished and famous architect, Philip Hardwick, the elder (1792–1870); and supplemented his training by three years of travel in Europe, where he visited the principal art galleries and museums, enlarging his knowledge of painting, sculpture and architecture. He fell in love with mediaeval building; the rich, flexible freedoms of Gothic animated his imagination, and determined the character of the furniture he designed. Although qualified as an architect, he never practiced; his creative abilities were devoted chiefly to designing furniture, and occasionally to interior fittings, wallpaper patterns, metalwork and jewellery. His merits and shortcomings as a designer are revealed by the illustrations of *Hints on Household Taste.*

The book was well received; reviewers were enthusiastic, and extracts from laudatory notices occupied the first two pages of the second edition, for the work was commercially successful, and in 1869 a second, revised edition was issued. The notice in *The Art Journal* was not quoted, possibly because it did not appear until the January issue, 1869. The reviewer had gently rebuked the author's "Gothic or mediaeval proclivities," but warmly recommended the book. Other reviewers had apparently shared the same thoughts, for in the preface to the second edition, Eastlake said: "Some of my critics have taken exception to what they not unjustifiably call my *mediaeval* predilections, and as there are not a few people to whom the very mention of Gothic furniture is very naturally associated with everything that is incommodius and pedantic, let me briefly explain what I had hoped would have been apparent to all who have read my book with attention, viz: — that I recommend the re-adoption of no specific type of ancient furniture which is unsuited, whether in detail or general design, to the habits of modern life. It is the spirit and principles of early manufacture which I desire to see revived, and not the absolute forms in which they found embodiment."

The last sentence reflects the ideas that motivated the handicraft revival, initiated by William Morris, which generated the Arts and Crafts movement. *Hints on Household Taste* made a potent contribution to the development of that movement. The book sold steadily; in 1878, ten years after its first appearance, a fourth revised and enlarged edition was published, from which the present reprint has been reproduced. In America the success of the book was considerable, and a so-called "Eastlake style" appeared, which the author disowned in his preface to the fourth edition when, with commendable restraint, he wrote: "I find American tradesmen continually advertising what they are pleased to call 'Eastlake' furniture, with the production of which I have had nothing whatever to do, and for the taste of which I should be very sorry to be considered responsible."

His book's popularity in the United States is attested by the number of editions; by 1881 six had been published; the "Eastlake Style" continued to benefit the American furniture trade, and travesties of his designs found their way into many American homes. Eastlake was a lucid writer, who explained his ideas simply, and never used technical jargon: his brisk common sense destroyed many established illusions about taste, especially those rooted in social snobbery. For example, in his Introduction, he observed that "The faculty of distinguishing good from bad design in the familiar objects of domestic life is a faculty which most educated people — and women especially — conceive that they possess. How it has been acquired, few would be able to explain. The general impression seems to be, that it is the peculiar inheritance of gentle blood, and independent of all training; that, while a young lady is devoting at school, or under a governess, so many hours a day to music, so many to languages, and so many to general science, she is all this time unconsciously forming that sense of the beautiful, which we call taste: that this sense, once developed, will enable her, unassisted by special study or experience, not only to appreciate the charms of nature in every aspect, but to form a correct estimate of the merits of art-manufacture" (page 8).

He knew that the designs he illustrated would disturb the visual complacency of the public. In the preface to the second edition he said: "I am aware that many of the sketches which I have supplied, as suggestive of reform in design, are unlike any objects in ordinary use. I should be sorry if they were not, believing, as I do, that most of our present household furniture is constructed on false principles. . . . If people of education would but lay aside the prejudices which have unfortunately become identified with the very name of a STYLE, and set themselves seriously to estimate the value of what was once a national and unperverted *tradition* in design, we might look more hopefully on the future of architecture, and the industrial arts of this country. As it is, our British amateurs are apt to range themselves under the respective standards of 'Gothic' and 'Classic'; and the result, it must be confessed, is on the whole not very advantageous to either cause."

That was written when the "Battle of the Styles" had raged for two generations; but Eastlake, although a Gothicist, recognised the futility of the conflict, and had no illusions about the character of mid-Victorian taste, which was based, he said, "upon eclecticism rather than on tradition," and was "capricious and subject to constant variation" (page 40). His unreserved admiration for the developing tradition of Gothic that had created a native English style in domestic architecture and furniture during the fifteenth and early sixteenth centuries never became an obsessive emotion; unlike his great contemporary, William Morris, he never allowed his love for mediaeval crafts and the skills of mediaeval craftsmen to embitter or distort his views about nineteenth-century life and industry, though he was sharply critical of the furniture manufacturing trade, and the growing traffic in faked antiques. He warned putative collectors of old furniture against the hucksters of Wardour

Street, which at that time was lined with curiosity shops, and told them that "as a rule, the 'Glastonbury' chairs and 'antique' book-cases sold in that venerable thoroughfare will prove on examination to be nothing but gross libels on the style of art which they are supposed to represent. A fragment of Jacobean wood-carving, or a single 'linen-fold' panel, is frequently considered a sufficient authority for the construction of a massive sideboard, which bears no more relation to the genuine work of the Middle Ages than the diaphanous paper of recent invention does to the stained-glass of our old cathedrals" (pages 64–65).

Eastlake was essentially a drawing-board designer; he was not an executant craftsman, like Morris, though he possessed an acute knowledge of the character of materials, derived from his practical training as an architect. His designs exhibit a structural frankness that barely avoids crudity, possibly because he lacked the "sense of touch" possessed by all craftsmen who think with their hands. He believed that if an article was strong and well-made, that its strength and structure should be obvious; so he used joined construction for his rather ponderous furniture, which was held together with pegged joints; glue was never used, nor were stains or polishes. "The present system of French-polishing, or literally *varnishing*, furniture is," he said, "destructive of all artistic effect in its appearance, because the surface of wood thus lacquered can never change its colour, or acquire that rich hue which is one of the chief charms of old cabinet-work" (pages 83–84).

He was well equipped to instruct the manufacturers who made furniture for him, and probably provided them with working drawings. A few makers, like Crace & Son, had, since the Great Exhibition of 1851, been producing furniture in the "Early English" or "Modern English Gothic" styles, as they were then known, and Eastlake's book gave fresh impetus and a new direction to these styles. In the first and second editions three of the plates illustrating furniture carried a line below the description, that read: "Executed from a Design by Charles L. Eastlake." Some of the furniture shown in the first two editions was omitted from the fourth, notably a library bookcase with marked Gothic affinities, a sloping top, and doors in the lower part with decorative strap hinges (Figure 1); also a design for a drawing room cheffonier (Figure 2) by the architect, Arthur William Blomfield* (1829–1899), who also contributed designs for wrought iron fenders, intended for a dining-room and a library. The fenders were retained, but Blomfield's cheffonier was dropped and replaced by the example on plate XXV, and the "Gothic" library bookcase was discarded in favour of the tall, well-proportioned and unpretentious design that

* He was knighted in 1899.

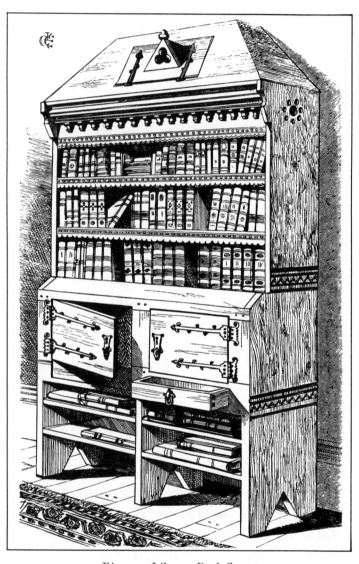

Fig. 1.   *Library Book Case*
executed from a design by Charles L. Eastlake.
This illustration appeared only in the first two editions of "Hints on
Household Taste."

Fig. 2.   *Drawing Room Cheffonier*
executed from a design by A. W. Blomfield.
Reproduced from the second edition of "Hints on Household Taste."

occupies plate XX. The designs on those two plates and several others added to the fourth edition were, according to the caption, "executed by Jackson & Graham," a famous West-end firm of cabinet-makers and furnishers. Their name appears in the royal accounts, and some of their work was shown at the Great Exhibition. Apart from the attributions on various plates, Eastlake states that the toilet table on page 213 and the wardrobe on page 217 were "executed by Messrs. Jackson and Graham," and though he implies that he designed them, does not specifically say so. On page 215 he reproduces one of his earlier designs for a chest of drawers with a toilet glass in a stout frame on it, which appeared in the first and second editions, and is wholly different in character from the Jackson and Graham toilet table and wardrobe. From the evidence of the new plates and text illustrations in the fourth edition, Eastlake had, apparently, simplified and refined his style, and pegged joints and mediaeval construction are not used in the pieces attributed to Jackson and Graham as makers.

Unfortunately no actual pieces made from Eastlake's designs have so far been traced, though Mr Christopher Hussey has described some furniture in a London house that was certainly influenced by the illustrations of his book.*

* *Country Life*, April 4, 1952, pages 996–999,

The house, Number 18, Stafford Terrace, on Campden Hill, Kensington, the residence of Mrs L. C. R. Messel, was originally furnished in 1874 for Linley Sambourne, the *Punch* cartoonist, who lived there until his death in 1910. An oak sideboard in one of the rooms is clearly derived from one of Eastlake's designs. It has inset panels on which Pre-Raphaelite sprays of fruit are painted against a gold background. One of the chairs resembles the illustration on page 175, which had been included in the early editions of *Hints on Household Taste*.

The outstanding characteristic of Eastlake's furniture is its simplicity; he relieved the massive form of his designs with appropriate ornament, and occasionally used turned members to enliven and emphasize vertical lines, as exemplified by the dining room sideboard on plate XI, and the drawing room cheffonier on plate XXV, for he greatly admired the art of the turner, and deplored its neglect. As survivals of the turner's skill, he cited the Windsor chair and the towel horse: "minor articles of household use which have been allowed to escape the innovations of modern taste. . . . A careful examination of these humble specimens of home manufacture will show that they are really superior in point of design to many pretentious elegancies of fashionable make" (pages 59–60). Although he advocated simplicity, and used ornament sparingly, his designs often lacked grace, and his chairs in particular had a loutish look, though they amply satisfied Victorian standards of comfort.

He mercilessly castigated current absurdities in fashion, such as the use of photographs for the lid and sides of coal boxes (pages 92–93), and said that "Every article of manufacture which is capable of decorative treatment should indicate, by its general design, the purpose to which it will be applied, and should never be allowed to convey a false notion of that purpose" (page 91). For the guidance of taste in a period that favoured excessive ornament, he condensed into fifteen words a basic principle: "In an age of debased design at least, the simplest style will be the best" (page 287). That advice is given in his last chapter on "Plate and Cutlery."

He is remembered chiefly as an author, for apart from the immensely popular *Hints on Household Taste*, he published in 1872 *A History of the Gothic Revival in England*, a work that established his reputation as an outstanding architectural historian. There were other minor works: in 1876 some talks he had delivered at the Social Science Congress appeared as *Lectures on Decorative Art and Art-Workmanship;* and during the eighteen eighties he produced a series of illustrated "Notes on the Principal Pictures," in various European art galleries: Brera Gallery, Milan, and the Louvre, Paris (1883); the old Pinakothek, Munich (1884); and the Royal Gallery, Venice (1888). His last published book, a series of social essays, appeared in 1895, entitled *Our Square and Circle*, which he signed with the name he had used in *The Queen* long before: "Jack Easel."

His professional career as an architect was confined to his work as Secretary of the R.I.B.A., from 1866 to 1878, a post he relinquished to become Keeper and Secretary of the National Gallery until 1898. (His uncle, Sir Charles Eastlake, had also been Keeper of the Gallery from 1843 to 1847, and Director in 1855.) During his period of office he rearranged and classified all the paintings in the collection.

He died in 1906, having in the course of an active and useful life opened the eyes of thousands of people, and made them aware of their surroundings and more critical of their possessions.

JOHN GLOAG

London
August, 1968

PREFACE.

In earlier editions of this book I expressed my hope
that a time would arrive when those who are chiefly
concerned with the control and management of industrial art in this country would perceive the necessity
of meeting a demand, which has existed for some time
past among our art-loving public, for improved taste in
objects of modern manufacture.

I am glad to find that hope at length realised—
if not to the full extent which I had anticipated—
at least as regards many branches of trade in which
the principles of good design had long been obsolete.

No one truly interested in such matters can fail
to have noticed the remarkable change which has
taken place within the last few years in the character
of domestic furniture, especially of cabinet work, textile fabrics, and pottery ; and although the benefit

of this change is occasionally marred by the ignorance of second-rate tradesmen, who, in their plagiarisms of good work, have missed the real spirit of its design, it is satisfactory to know that some of the oldest and most reputable firms of manufacturers in London, Manchester, and Birmingham, are seeking advice and assistance from competent designers, with a result which has a directly beneficial influence on the nature of their productions.

Of course it will take some time before this influence will extend to that unfortunately large class of the British public who are indifferent to art of any kind, and who only care to secure 'novelties' (which may be as remarkable for ugliness as beauty) in furnishing their homes. But, inasmuch as the number of artistically appointed houses is steadily increasing, it is to be hoped that those who have had no opportunity of forming a judgment on such matters will by degrees take their cue from others of more cultivated taste.

The progress of industrial art is not likely to be arrested by the narrow prejudice of those whose perceptions of beauty in human handiwork are strictly limited to the fields of painting and sculpture, nor by the sneers of ignorant critics who imagine that every departure from the conventional type of chair or table in ordinary use must necessarily be attended by personal inconvenience.

It is true that when the attention of the public was first directed to this subject, the furniture of the day was of such a vulgar and extravagant kind, that those who advocated a reform in this department of art were tempted to recommend a return to the earliest and most archaic types of design, as an escape from the evil which they denounced. But study and experience have since proved that the internal fittings of a house may be made picturesque and interesting without being rude and clumsy in form, and that it is not necessary to sacrifice the refinements and comfort to which we are accustomed in the nineteenth century, in order to secure simplicity of style.

In revising this volume for the press, I have taken the opportunity to replace some of the original illustrations by others more representative of the advance which has lately been made in the character of contemporary manufacture.

I would, however, caution my readers against supposing that any designs represented on such a small scale as in the following wood-cuts, can serve as correct models for reproduction by upholsterers and cabinet-makers, without the working drawings necessary for their proper execution ; and I think it the more necessary to state this, as I find American tradesmen continually advertising what they are pleased to call ' Eastlake' furniture, with the production of which I have had nothing whatever to do, and for the taste of which I should be very sorry to be considered responsible.

The only detailed designs I have made for furniture (beyond those supplied to private clients) have been for a few English firms, most of whose names are mentioned in this book, and to whom of course the copyright of such designs belongs.

CHARLES L. EASTLAKE.

41 LEINSTER SQUARE,
BAYSWATER, W.

CONTENTS.

———◆———

ILLUSTRATIONS.

Plates V, VI, VII, VIII, XIV, XV, XVI, XVII and XVIII were reproduced in color in the 1878 edition. In this reprint these plates are reproduced in the appropriate places in black and white.

Introduction.

I T is unfortunate for the interests of Art at the present time that in civilised countries it has come to be regarded as the result of theories utterly remote from the question of ordinary taste, totally distinct from those principles which influence manufacture and structural science, and independent of any standard of excellence which we might expect to be derived from common sense. Let us suppose, for instance, a man of good education, accustomed to associate with well-bred people from his youth, but who had never chanced to reckon a painter among his intimate friends, and had acquired no more knowledge of pictures than what it is possible to gather from books and newspapers, taken for the first time in his life to a second-rate modern exhibition, and afterwards to the collection of old masters which now forms our National Gallery. Can anyone doubt for a moment that he would prefer the most literal representations of contemporary life to the ideal and frequently conventional treatment of the classic schools? He would see little or no merit in the glowing colours of Titian, the flowing draperies of Veronese, the broad handling of Velasquez, the careful detail of Van Eyck. But the cheapest form of sentiment embodied in a modern picture, so long as it seemed to realise scenes, incidents, and action which he was accustomed to see about him, would at once appeal to his imagination and interest his eye.

This commonplace taste was, until lately, not confined to pictorial art. If we may believe those who have given their attention to the subject of technical design, it pervaded and vitiated the judgment by which we were accustomed to select and approve the objects of everyday use in our houses. It crossed our path in the Brussels carpet of our drawing-rooms ; it was about our beds in the shape of gaudy chintz ; it compelled us to rest on chairs and to sit at tables which were designed in accordance with the worst principles of construction and invested with shapes confessedly unpicturesque. It sent us metal-work from

Birmingham which was as vulgar in form as it was flimsy in execution. It decorated the finest modern porcelain with the most objectionable character of ornament. It lined our walls with silly representations of vegetable life, or with a mass of uninteresting diaper. It bade us, in short, furnish our houses after the same fashion as we dress ourselves, and that is with no more sense of real beauty than if art were a dead letter.

It is hardly necessary to say that the general public did not recognise this fact. In the eyes of Mater-familias there was no upholstery which could possibly surpass that which the most fashionable upholsterer supplied. She believed in the elegance of window-curtains, of which so many dozen yards had been sent to the Duchess of ——, and concluded that the dinner-service must be perfect which was described as 'quite a novelty.' When did people first adopt the monstrous notion that the 'last pattern out' must be the best? Is good taste so rapidly progressive that every mug which leaves the potter's hands surpasses in shape the last which he moulded? Far from this, it is to be feared that, instead of progressing, we have, for some ages at least, gone hopelessly backward in the arts of manufacture. And this is true not only with respect to the character of design, but often in regard to the actual quality of material employed. It is generally admitted by every housewife who has attained a matronly age, that linen, silk, and other articles of textile fabric, though less expensive than formerly, are far inferior to what was made in the days of our grandfathers. Metal-workers tell us that it is almost impossible to procure, for the purpose of their trade, brass such as appears to have been in common use a century ago. Joinery is neither so sound nor so artistic as it was in the early Georgian era. A cheap and easy method of workmanship—an endeavour to produce a show of finish with the least possible labour, and, above all, an unhealthy spirit of competition in regard to price, such as was unknown to previous generations—have combined to deteriorate the value of our ordinary mechanics' work.

Now although in the field of art, as well as in the researches of science, it is not always easy for the uninitiated to determine of two collateral phenomena, which may be referred to cause and which to effect, it must be evident to all who have thought earnestly on the subject, that there is an intimate connection between this falling off in the excellence of our manufactures, and the tame vapid character which distinguished even our best painters' work in the early part of the present Victorian age. Doubtless in this particular epoch there have been individual instances of men who, like Turner, created a new impulse in some special branch of their profession—just as Wedgwood distinguished himself by his strenuous efforts to throw fresh life and vigour into the system of ceramic design ; but these are solitary cases, and can hardly be quoted as indicative of a generally advancing taste. National art is not a thing which we may inclose in a gilt frame and hang upon our walls, or which can be locked up in the cabinet of a collector. To be genuine and permanent, it ought to animate with the same spirit the blacksmith's forge and the sculptor's *atelier*, the painter's studio and the haberdasher's shop. In the great ages of art it was so. Francia, a carpenter's son, was brought up as a *niello* engraver. He became a great painter, but he was not for that reason ashamed to work at decorating jewellery. He loved to sign his pictures 'Aurifex,' and on his trinkets he inscribed the word 'Pictor.' The most liberal salary which Messrs. Hunt and Roskell might be prepared to pay would not secure such assistance now. Modern jewellers, as a rule, know nothing of pictorial art ; painters, it is to be feared, have but little taste in jewellery. Every branch of manufacture is inclosed within its own limits —has its own particular style. Our china, which once imitated Oriental ware, not long ago promised to assume, through Minton's influence, a quasi-mediæval character. The goldsmiths who once produced nothing but rococo ornaments have since endeavoured to imitate Etruscan necklaces and armlets. We had French mirrors and Persian rugs, Greek vases and Roman lamps—designs of every age and country but our own; or if by some chance we could point to any special instance of a genuine English design, it was generally mean and uninteresting.

As this was especially the case with those articles of household use on which the eye had constantly to rest, we can scarcely be surprised that there was so little popular sympathy with works of high aim in pictorial art. People fell into a way of ridiculing things as 'quaint' and 'peculiar' which happened to differ from the conventional ugliness of the modern drawing-room. When crinoline, for instance, was in the height of its fashion, any young lady who had the courage to appear without it would have been called a 'fright' in regard to her toilet, without reference to the patent fact that her dress, allowed to fall into natural folds, disposed itself much more gracefully than when stretched over the steel hoop, which, happily for us, is once more trundled into oblivion. Now, if we reflect on the baneful influence which this wretched invention must have had some years ago on the tastes of the rising generation, and how children grew up in the belief that it actually lent a sort of charm to the skirts of their mothers' dresses, we shall feel less surprised at the apathy and want of appreciation with which the Venus of Milo, or the drapery of any other antique statue, is regarded by young women of fashion at the present day. In the same way, if we contemplate with satisfaction—nay, if we even tolerate the extravagant and graceless appointments of the modern boudoir, let us not be surprised that we find it mirrored on the modern canvas. The most natural instinct of the painter's mind is, after all, to depict life as he finds it; and in all the best ages of art this was practically done, even by those whose aim tended towards the ideal. Phidias, Raphael, and (if we venture to place their names together) Hogarth may here be said to meet on common ground. We can hardly hope then, in our own time, to sustain anything like a real and national interest in art while we tamely submit to ugliness in modern manufacture. We cannot consistently have one taste for the drawing-room and another for the studio; but, perhaps, the

best discipline which could be devised for the latter
would be initiated by a thorough reform of the first.

The faculty of distinguishing good from bad design
in the familiar objects of domestic life is a faculty
which most educated people—and women especially—
conceive that they possess.   How it has been acquired,
few would be able to explain.   The general impression
seems to be, that it is the peculiar inheritance of gentle
blood, and independent of all training ; that, while a
young lady is devoting at school, or under a governess,
so many hours a day to music, so many to languages,
and so many to general science, she is all this time unconsciously forming that sense of the beautiful, which
we call taste : that this sense, once developed, will
enable her, unassisted by special study or experience,
not only to appreciate the charms of nature in every
aspect, but to form a correct estimate of the merits of
art-manufacture.   That this impression has gained
ground so far as to amount to positive conviction, may
be inferred from the fact that there is no single point
on which well-bred women are more jealous of dispar-
agement than on this.   We may condemn a lady's
opinion on politics—criticise her handwriting—correct
her pronunciation of Latin, and disparage her favourite
author with a chance of escaping displeasure.   But if

we venture to question her taste—in the most ordinary
sense of the word, we are sure to offend. It is, however, a lamentable fact that this very quality was until
recently deficient, not only among the generally ignorant, but also among the most educated classes in this
country. How could it be otherwise? Even the
simplest and most elementary principles of decorative
art form no part of early instruction, and the majority
of the public, being left completely uninformed of them,
is content to be guided by a few people who are themselves not only uninformed but misinformed on the
subject. It is scarcely too much to say that ninety-nine
out of every hundred English gentlewomen who have
the credit of dressing well depend entirely upon their
milliners for advice as to what they may, and what they
may not, wear. The latest novelty from Paris is recommended, not because it has any special merit on
the score of artistic beauty, but simply because it is a
novelty. Of course it would be useless to urge, in
answer to this, that a certain form of dress, once
accepted as good, must always be good; or to deny
that a particular combination of colours, recognised as
harmonious, can become discordant, simply because it
does not appear in the pages of *Le Follet.* Unfortunately, the world of fashion is so constituted that people

who move in it are obliged to conform more or less to its rules ; and as no lady likes to make herself conspicuous by her dress, she may reasonably abstain from wearing what has been long out of date. But there is a limit to all things ; and the capricious tyranny which insists on a monthly change of style ought to be firmly resisted by women who are too sensible to give up their whole time and attention to their toilet. Of course it is the interest of milliners to multiply these changes as frequently as possible, and the waste of money thus incurred (to say nothing of higher considerations) has been a just cause of complaint with many a husband and father. Leaving the moral aspect of the matter, however, out of the question, it must be confessed that to hear a young shopman defining to his fair customers across the counter what is ' genteel ' or ' ladylike,' sounds very ludicrous, and even impertinent. Yet in this sort of advice apparently lies the only guiding principle of their selection. They choose not what they like best, but what is ' very much worn,' or what their obsequious adviser recommends them as suitable.

Counsel of such a kind, and the easy confidence in its worth, are, unfortunately, not confined to the haberdasher's shop. They seem inseparable from the purchase of every article which, from the nature of its design or manufacture, can claim to be of an ornamental character. When Materfamilias enters an ordinary upholsterer's warehouse, how can she possibly decide on the pattern of her new carpet, when bale after bale of Brussels is unrolled by the indefatigable youth, who is equal in his praises of every piece in turn ? Shall it be the ' House of Lords ' diaper, of a yellow spot upon a blue ground ; or the ' imitation Turkey,' with its multifarious colours ; or the beautiful new *moiré* design ; or yonder exquisite invention of green fern-leaves, tied up with knots of white satin ribbon ?* The shopman remarks of one piece of goods that it is ' elegant ' ; of another, that it is ' striking ' ; of a third, that it is ' unique,' and so forth. The good lady looks from one carpet to another until her eyes are fairly dazzled by their hues. She is utterly unable to explain why she should, or why she should not, like any of them. Perhaps a friend is appealed to, who, being a strong-minded person (with the additional incentive of a wish to bring the matter to an issue as speedily as possible), at once selects the very pattern which Materfamilias pronounced to be ' a

---

* This preposterous pattern has not only been employed for carpets, but was once very popular, and may be noticed as an instance of the degradation to which the arts of design can descend.

fright' only two minutes ago. In this dilemma the gentleman with the yard-wand again comes to the rescue, states his firm opinion as to which is most 'fashionable,' and this at once carries the day. The carpet is made up, sent home, and takes its chance of domestic admiration together with all other household appointments. It may kill by its colour every piece of *tapisserie* in the room. It may convey the notion of a bed of roses, or a dangerous labyrinth of rococo ornament—but if it is 'fashionable,' that is all-sufficient. While new, it is admired; when old, everybody will agree that it was always 'hideous.'

Glass, china, table-linen, window-curtains, tables, chairs, and cabinet-work, used all to be chosen on this plan. The latest invention, although it might violate every principle of good design, was sure to be a favourite with the majority. An article which dated from a few years back was rejected as old-fashioned. This absurd love of change—simply for the sake of change, is even now carried to such an extent that if one desires to replace a jug or a table-cloth with another of the same pattern, even a few months after the first has been bought, however good the style may have been, it is extremely difficult, sometimes impossible, to do so. The answer is always the same :

'Last year's goods, sir; we couldn't match them now.'

This state of things is the fault, not only of the manufacturer, but of the purchaser. So long as a thirst for mere novelty exists independently of all artistic considerations, the aim at Manchester and Sheffield will be to produce objects which, by their singular form, or striking combination cf colours, shall always appear *new*. From such an endeavour some originality indeed resulted, but also a vast deal of ugliness. Now and then a good thing found its way into the sale-room or shop-window, struck the fancy of some buyer, and was sent home. But if we searched for the same article next season, we probably found that it had been condemned to make room for some trash, which was in request for no better reason than because nothing like it had appeared before.

For many years past there has been, as I have said, a great deficiency in public taste on such points, but by degrees people are beginning to awaken to the fact, that there is a right and a wrong notion of taste in upholstery, in jewellery—perhaps in millinery, too— and in many other fields which stand apart from a connoisseurship of what is commonly called 'high art.' The revival of ecclesiastical decoration, for instance,

has called ladies' attention to the subject of embroidery ;
and they are relinquishing the ridiculous custom of
endeavouring to reproduce, in cross-stitch worsted-
work, the pictures of Landseer and Frank Stone.
There is a growing impatience of paperhangings which
would beguile the unwary into a shadowy suspicion
that the drawing-room walls are fitted up with trellis-
work for training Brobdignag convolvuli ; and portraits of the once-celebrated Bengal tiger no longer
appear on the domestic hearth-rug.   The modern
fashion of dining *à la Russe* has given a new impulse
to the manufacture of dessert services and table-glass ;
and the improved education of students in the schools
of design has been attended with beneficial results in
more quarters than one.   Still there seems to be a
great want of popular information for the guidance of
those who have neither time nor inclination to study
the abstruse works on various departments of decorative art which have from time to time appeared in this
country.

It is hoped, therefore, that a few familiar hints on
what may be called ' household taste' will not be un-
acceptable to the readers of this book.   There is a
class of young ladies who are in the habit of anticipat-
ing all differences of opinion in a picture-gallery or

concert-room by saying that they 'know what they like.' Whatever advantage may be derived from this remarkable conviction in regard to music or painting, I fear it would assist no one in furnishing a house—at least, in accordance with any established principles of art. It will be my endeavour, in the following chapters, to point out those principles, so far as they have been laid down by writers of acknowledged authority, taking care to avoid all technical details in regard to manufacture, which, however interesting to the specialist, would be useless to the general reader; and if I am thus enabled, even indirectly, to encourage a discrimination between good and bad design in those articles of daily use which we are accustomed to see around us, my object will be attained.

Chapter I.

STREET ARCHITECTURE.

IT is always interesting to note the early impressions which the superficial aspect of our country produces on foreigners who visit it for the first time, and to compare those impressions with feelings such as we have ourselves experienced under similar conditions on the Continent. After making every allowance for the charm of novelty, which of course goes far to enhance a stranger's enjoyment on these occasions, we cannot doubt that there is much in the external appearance of foreign life which possesses especial attractions for our countrymen. The first glimpse, for instance, which we get, after crossing the Channel, of such a town as Dieppe, or the gratification which we derive from wandering for the first time through the streets of a city like Nuremburg, whose general aspect has remained almost unaltered since the Middle Ages, is associated with a sense of what may be called eye-pleasure, which is utterly

Street in Nuremberg.

absent in our English provincial towns. The latter may be better paved, cleaner swept, and more expensively laid out than their French or German rivals ; but they are for the most part utterly wanting in one important element of architectural merit—viz. the picturesque. When we pass on to compare the capital of France with our own metropolis, a still wider difference is discernible, though from causes of another kind. Modern Paris is fast losing—if, indeed, it has not quite lost—the romantic interest which once attached to its *genius loci.* The quaint irregularly built streets, the overhanging corbelled stories and high-pitched gable-fronts which rise before us as we read ' The Hunchback of Notre Dame,' and which lingered down to the days of Smollett, and even to our own time, have suddenly disappeared before the rapid and extensive improvements which were carried on under the late Imperial Government.

Anyone who has traced on an old map of Paris the labyrinth of dark and narrow streets through which the Rue de Rivoli has boldly cut, or who can remember the former aspect of those quarters now intersected by the Boulevart Sebastopol, and other thoroughfares, will bear witness to the almost magical effect of a transformation which the social economist or the sanitary commissioner indeed may view with satisfaction, but which the artist and antiquary cannot but deplore. The architecture of modern Paris is by no means all that a man of sound taste can approve. It is cold and formal in general effect. In detail it is somewhat garish, but more often simply uninteresting. The long unbroken line of cornice, window-range, or parapet, which presents itself to the eye in interminable perspective, becomes wearisome even in the widest and loftiest of streets. Yet, right or wrong, there is a uniformity of purpose, a character and completeness about the work, which not only bears the impress of a national taste, but exhibits the influence of some direct and competent supervision. Unfortunately in England we can boast of no national taste in architecture, and the scheme on which our Executive Government is based prevents anything like State interference regarding the design of buildings devoted to private enterprise or occupation. So every householder or merchant builds according to his own fancy, or rather according to the fancy of the professional gentleman whom he employs to plan his villa or his warehouse.

Of course I am now alluding to the best structures of each class. As for the myriads of cockney cottages, suburban streets, tawdry shop-fronts, and stuccoed terraces, which are rising up in the outskirts of London, they speak for themselves; and as long as people of humble means will insist on assuming the semblance of luxuries which they cannot really afford, vulgarities of design and structural deceits must prevail in this direction. But where there is no stint of means—where the work, if done at all, should, and might easily be done well, and where, under these conditions, we find taste neglected, and money thrown away, the result is indeed melancholy to contemplate.

Perhaps the most consistent phase of modern street architecture in London is that which has appeared in connection with the West-end clubs. Yet these, as a rule, are but copies, and, not unfrequently, vitiated copies, of actual buildings illustrating an exotic school of art which had never a footing in England until our own had been lost or degraded. The so-called Italian style—now understood to include every variety of Renaissance design which prevailed in Rome, Venice, and Florence, from the sixteenth to the eighteenth century—has its æsthetic merits and its practical advantages. But they are merits and advantages which are unsuited to the age, to the climate, and to the country in which they are reproduced. It does not require the judgment of an accomplished connois-

seur to perceive that mouldings and carved enrich-
ments which look well under the glowing effect of a
Venetian sky, must appear tame and spiritless through
the leaden atmosphere of London. We want in
England a less refined and more nervous expression
of architectural beauty — bold and sturdy features,
which will hold their own against wind and rain, and
defy the smoke and traffic of our busy coal-burning
towns. But it is not often that we can complain with
any reason of undue refinement in our imitations of
Italian architecture. Even those which are confessedly
copied from old examples miss, either intentionally or
through inaccurate workmanship, the delicacy of the
original design. And, in too many instances, where
our architects have ignored the value of precedent, and
struck out a new line for themselves, the result has
been hopelessly clumsy or *bizarre.* It is only by a
long and careful course of study, based on naturally
good and inventive taste, that these mistakes can be
avoided on the part of the designer. And it is only
by the well-directed and long-sustained efforts of
designers that the British public will ever be brought
to distinguish good from bad in modern architecture.
Ignorant amateurs of the art may be divided into two
classes—those who have a smattering of book lore on

the subject, and who think no building worth looking at which is not based on 'authority,' or, in other words, which is not copied from some existing work ; and those who have a morbid craving after novelty at the expense of every other consideration, including that invaluable standard of architectural fitness which is supplied by common sense.

It is to the first of these two classes that we are indebted for the encouragement and support of the pseudo-classicism with which, in the form of churches, clubs, and public institutions, London was deluged in the early part of this century. The tide of public favour afterwards turned in an opposite direction ; and while all must admit the laudable zeal with which Pugin and his followers endeavoured to revive old English architecture in this country, it is lamentable to reflect how many monstrous designs were per-petrated under the general name of Gothic, which neither in spirit nor letter realised the character of mediæval art. In London these extraordinary ebulli-tions of uneducated taste generally appear in the form of meeting-houses, music-halls, and similar places of popular resort. Showy in their general effect, and usually overloaded with meretricious ornament, they are likely enough to impose upon an uninformed judg-

ment, which is incapable of discriminating between
what Mr. Ruskin has called the Lamp of Sacrifice—
one of the glories of ancient art—and the lust of profusion which is the bane of modern design. These
extravagances are not confined to a perversion of
Gothic. Some of the 'Monster' hotels, railway stations,
and other buildings of a type unknown to our forefathers, but now erected in London, are decorated
after a fashion which is equally novel, and which has
nothing but novelty to recommend it. But then most
of these buildings are six or seven stories high, make
up so many hundred beds, and are managed by a host
who is so important a personage that we never see him
at all! These facts, doubtless, enhance our respect for
an establishment which, on a smaller scale, might be
open to some criticism on the ground both of personal
convenience and of artistic propriety.

Some attempts at architectural display are occasionally made in the way of shop-fronts. But here a
certain practical difficulty attends the designer. However elegant the superstructure may be, it has one
drawback; it must rest on nothing, or, at least, apparently on nothing; the aim of every modern retail
dealer being to expose his goods for sale behind a
single sheet of plate glass. In accordance with this

object—for which no explanation can ever be given except that it is universal—iron columns are furtively introduced, and as carefully concealed by millinery, upholstery, or sometimes by craftily-contrived mirrors, so that when all is finished the upper portion of the building seems absolutely suspended in the air. Such conditions are not exactly fitted for ordinary treatment of design; yet the shop-front architect delights in ignoring them altogether, and in loading his upper stories with pediments, columns, niches, and cornices, just as if they stood on a basement as solid as that of the Pitti Palace. It seems astonishing that the old practice of turning a sound arch or placing a real lintel over every shop-window should have fallen into such disuse. Yet so seldom is this done, and so much does the objectionable practice of using iron columns and girders in such places prevail, that some blocks of newly re-built shops at the west-end of Oxford-street, on the Marquis of Westminster's estate, are quite conspicuous as an exception—and in this respect a creditable exception—to the general rule.

Of the dwelling-houses in London, those which have any pretension to architectural design are few in number, and lie chiefly in the neighbourhood of the parks or of the oldest West-end squares. But the ordinary residences of fashionable life—the mansions of Belgravia, Tyburnia, and Mayfair—are mere shells of brick and stucco, which present such a dreary appearance outside that one is surprised sometimes to find them palaces of comfort within.

The Frenchman who expressed his opinion that London had ceased to be a town, and was becoming a vast province, uttered no mere hyperbole. Between the years 1800 and 1860 this metropolis not only doubled, but trebled, the size which it had assumed at the close of the last century. At the present time, including the suburbs, it occupies a superficial area of at least 130 square miles. On an average, about 1,000 houses are added to it every year; and so rapidly does building go on in every direction, that no one need be surprised to find the meadow-land which he walked on in spring laid out in populous streets by Christmas. There is, however, a great difference between the gradual development of the old city and the additions which we make to our modern capital. When Bloomsbury was still a fashionable district, its inhabitants no doubt regarded it as a permanent enlargement of London, and looked forward to the time when their children's children might own the tenements which they bought or rented. That is a source of prospective pleasure in which the inhabitants of Belgravia and Tyburnia cannot indulge. According to the present system of tenure adopted for house property, the rule is to build residences which are only intended to last a certain number of years. At the end of that term they fall into the possession of the landowner on whose estate they are erected, and thus it is to the interest of his tenant (who, in nine cases out of ten, is a speculating builder) not to spend more money on their construction than is absolutely necessary.*

This is an unsatisfactory state of things even in a *primâ facie* view of the matter. To calculate the stability of a house so nicely that at the expiration of, say, seventy years, it shall only be fit to be pulled down and sold for old materials, is a method of reckoning which obviously involves some discomfort, not to say danger, to its latest occupant. But, unfortunately, this is not the extent of the evil. In the earnest endeavour to avoid the expense of an unnecessary stability, these economists too frequently err on the side of weakness. To speak plainly, it will be a

---

* The recently revived taste for the so-called 'Queen Anne' style, or more correctly speaking for that domestic type of brick architecture which prevailed, with certain variations, from the Caroline to the Georgian period, has resulted in the erection in London of many private mansions which are very picturesque, and which reflect great credit on the architects who designed them.

miracle if half the houses which are now being raised
in and about London do not, in the ordinary course of
things, tumble down long before their allotted time.
Unfortunately, their flimsy construction is not always
apparent to an inexperienced eye. The old brick
mansions of the early Georgian era, although unpretentious in appearance, were at least as strong as good
burnt clay and duly mixed mortar could make them ;
the walls were of substantial thickness ; the timber
was dry, sound, and of ample dimensions ; the founda-
tions were well laid ; the roof was of a convenient
pitch and covered with the best of slates ; the doors
were securely hung, and a true lintel or a real arch,
with properly tapering *voussoirs*, was turned over every
window. The woodwork and fittings of these houses,
though modelled in a pseudo-classic taste, were excellent in workmanship, and frequently spirited in detail ;
while the wrought iron introduced to decorate their
façades in the shape of gates and area-railings is
designed in thorough accordance with the nature and
properties of the material employed. The truth is,
that in those days, inferior or dishonest work would
soon have been detected, for there was nothing to
conceal it from public view. Plaster was of course
used internally, as it had been during centuries past,

III.

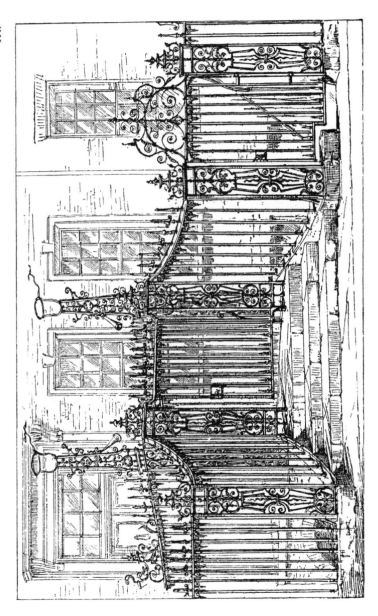

Area Railings
of a House in Great Ormond Street, Bloomsbury.

for the sake of convenience and cleanliness ; but no one had yet conceived the idea of coating the front of a brick house with a composition which should give it the appearance of masonry. In an evil hour *stucco* was invented ; and thenceforth, wherever it was employed, good and bad work was reduced, in the eyes of the general public, to one common level. It mattered little whether brick or rubble, English or Flemish bond were used ; whether the courses exceeded their proper height by a dangerous preponderance of mortar; whether the openings were really arched over or only spanned by a fictitious lintel. What signified such considerations as these when the whole front was to be enveloped in a fair and specious mask of cement ?

How far this detestable practice has increased in London anyone familiar with the principal suburban squares and streets can well testify. But what the general public do *not* know is that the structural deceits which it conceals are daily becoming so numerous and flagrant that they positively endanger life and property. How frequently have we heard, during the last few years, of the fall of houses which have been built even within the recollection of the rising generation ? The only wonder is that these casualties do not happen every day. Of course, when an accident has occurred, the district surveyor is called in as a responsible agent to give evidence before the authorities of the state in which the house was when he last examined it. But this examination is too frequently a mere matter of form. It is the surveyor's business to arrest and remedy any gross violation of the Building Act. But in a populous and suburban district, where houses are being run up (as the phrase is) in all directions, it is impossible for him to be in all places at once, or attempt to keep up a constant supervision. Besides, in the matter of bricklaying, as in all other concerns of life, it is very easy to keep within the letter of the law and at the same time disregard its spirit.

The Building Act itself, though framed in such a manner as to exclude many picturesque features from a London street, is on the whole rather lenient on the subject of roof-scantlings and the dimensions of a party wall. An architect who should attempt to add to the effect of his elevation by a bay-window looking into the street or by overhanging eaves (even provided with a gutter) would find himself somewhat impeded by existing legislation. Yet a heavy 'compo' cornice, barely strong enough to support itself, is allowed to project a considerable distance from the front wall, daily threatening the lives of passers-by ; and a miserable lintel, composed of fragments of brick, stuck together with mortar in the weakest possible form, is often used under the name of a ' flat arch.'

These are only a few of the legalised evils of modern house building. As for those which are forgotten, overlooked, or winked at, their number is legion. Not only is plaster or cement used as a covering for inferior brickwork, but it is boldly employed for columns, parapets, and verandah balusters in place of stone. It is not at all an uncommon thing to see a would-be Doric or Corinthian shaft shorn of its base, and actually hanging to the side of a house until the pedestal (which, of course, will also be of cement) is completed. Plaster brackets support plaster pediments : stucco bas-reliefs are raised upon a stucco ground. The whole front is a sham, from the basement story to the attics. But murder will out, and by degrees this prodigious imposition begins to reveal itself. A mouldy green dampness exudes from the hastily finished walls. The ill-fated stucco blisters up and peels off in all directions. Ugly fissures appear on the house-front, caused by some 'settlement,' arising from bad founda- tions. The wretched parodies on carved work become chipped away by accident, or crumble to fragments

under the influence of the weather.   There is an air of
shabby gentility about the whole structure which would
be ludicrous if it were not pitiable.   It had only a
meretricious excellence when fresh from the painter's
hands.   A few years have made it a dingy abode : a
few more years will make it a ghastly ruin.

The interior arrangements are not a whit better.
Floor-boards come up unexpectedly after separating
from the skirting ; doors shrink so that they cannot be
securely fastened ; window-sashes warp and become im-
movable; marble chimney-pieces are gradually detached
from the wall behind them.   In short, the external dis-
order only foreshadows internal discomfort.   Of course,
when houses of this class are intrusted to efficient hands,
under the management of an honest builder, the case
is very different ; but, judging from the average condition of what are called second-class dwelling-houses,
I believe that I have drawn no exaggerated picture of
their state.

The shop-fronts of London indicate a still greater
disregard of the first principles of construction.   In
former days, when the British tradesman's place of
business and residence were under the same roof, a
modest display of goods was deemed sufficient for the
ground-floor, and nowise interfered with the stability

of the superstructure : but at the present time, when each draper and silversmith wants to make a greater show than his neighbour, all semblance of strength is banished from the street level. Everything is given up to plate glass. Now plate glass is an excellent material in its way, but we cannot expect it to support three or four stories of solid brickwork. To meet this requirement, therefore, iron columns and iron girders are introduced, and, as artistic effect must yield to the stern necessities of commercial life, it would be idle to urge any but practical objections to the system. Such objections, however, are not wanting. The nature and properties of iron, although well studied by scientific engineers, are but imperfectly understood by the public. In addition to the chance of a flaw in the casting, or any of those more obvious contingencies to which stone and wood are also subject, one fact stands pre-eminently forward. Every schoolboy knows that iron expands with heat and contracts with cold. Let us suppose any large mansion in Belgravia, or a West-end draper's establishment, attacked by fire ; iron has been profusely introduced in its construction, and is affected in the ordinary way ; the engines arrive and distribute water over the premises. Can any one doubt what the result would be ? The ironwork thus suddenly

cooled must, of necessity, be liable to fracture ; and if
the whole building tumbles to the ground, it need be
no matter of surprise to those who are acquainted with
the secret of its structure.

It is quite time that these evils should be remedied
by legislation. It would not be difficult to strengthen
the case by artistic considerations, but in the main the
question assumes a practical form. It is unpleasant to
live within ugly walls ; it is still more unpleasar.t to live
within unstable walls ; but to be obliged to live in a
tenement which is both unstable and ugly is disagree-
able in a tenfold degree. An Englishman's house was
formerly said to be his castle. But in the hands of the
speculating builder and advertising tradesman, we may
be grateful that it does not oftener become his tomb.

It is true that within the last few years attempts have
here and there been made to invest our street architecture—so far as shops and warehouses are concerned—
with more character and stability. And this is mainly
owing to the revival of a style which, however modified by the influence of climate and national habits in
the various countries where it prevailed, was everywhere distinguished by a uniform honesty of constructive purpose. The Gothic Renaissance may seem a
paradoxical teim to use, but in a literal sense it may

be fairly applied to that Reformation in the style of
national architecture, which required *sound construction*
as a primary condition of excellence in house-building.

The art-historian who, in a future age, shall attempt
to describe the various phases of taste through which
English painting and architecture have passed during
this century, will have no easy task before him. If
the march of science has been rapid, it has also been
steady, and marked by events and discoveries which
will enable posterity to distinguish between true and
false theory, real progress, and futile digression. But
no such landmarks exist to indicate the several roads
by which we have arrived, or hope to arrive, at æsthetic greatness in the reign of Queen Victoria. The
ancient highways of art are seldom traversed. Our
modern geniuses have struck out new paths for themselves, which here and there cross, indeed, the course
of their predecessors, but rarely coincide with it.
These are so diverse in their direction that they may
be said to have formed a sort of labyrinth which by
and by it will be difficult to survey.

That this should be the case regarding pictorial
art is not surprising. Before the time of Hogarth we
never had a national school of painting ; and even our
modern English styles have derived more from foreign

teaching than they have inherited from Hogarth. But a national architecture we did once possess. How much of its spirit was actually indigenous—how much was introduced by the Normans, and how much it subsequently owed to external influences, we may leave the antiquaries to settle. It is sufficient to know that, during at least four centuries of English history, our houses, castles, churches, and country mansions, were designed in a fashion which was as characteristic of this country as the dress and manners, if not the language, of the people. Then came the decadence or decline of mediæval art, which was followed by a revival of classic design, modified to suit the requirements of modern life. It took its rise in Italy, and spread gradually over the whole of Western Europe. Its influence was at first only partially felt in this country. Long after Florence had raised her palaces of the Pitti, the Pandolfini, and the Strozzi; long after Raphael had completed the stately basilica which Bramante had begun for modern Rome; long after Venice and Verona could boast of a splendid Renaissance, English architecture continued in a degraded state of transition between the two styles. It had lost the purity of ancient Gothic. It had not yet developed the principles of Italian design. The result

Window in Dining-room at Cothele, Devon.

was a miserable compromise, by which classic details of the clumsiest description were grafted on buildings supported by the Tudor arch, and crowned with the Tudor gable. It is, perhaps, the bizarre and picturesque character of this bastard style which still renders it popular with the uneducated. To this day Elizabethan mansions are admired by sentimental young ladies (who, by the way, generally call them Elizabeth*ian*) as the perfection of architectural taste. But the truth is, whatever real elements of beauty belonged to English architecture in the sixteenth century, were possessed in a tenfold degree by the style which preceded and the style which followed that epoch. Inigo Jones appears to have been the first of our countrymen who designed Italian with real purity. Even he in his earlier days did not altogether abandon Gothic. But the tide of public taste had now begun to turn. The fire of London opened a wide field for the genius of Wren ; and from the rebuilding of St. Paul's Cathedral down to the accession of Queen Victoria every building of importance raised in England has been either Italian in character, or a modified adaptation of that style.

It would be hazardous to ascribe to any special cause or influence the change of popular sentiment which has since taken place with regard to architecture in this country. We may, however, not unreasonably infer that it was in a great measure brought about by the new impulse which English literature received in the early part of the present century. Indeed such an influence would not be without precedent. It was the revival of classic letters which induced the imitation of classic art. It was the love of mediæval lore, of Old English traditions, of border chivalry, which, by the magic power of association, led the more romantic of our sires and grandsires first to be interested in Gothic architecture, and then to discern its beauties. Horace Walpole, both as an author and a *virtuoso*, may be said to have sown the seeds of this taste, but it is to the writings of Sir Walter Scott that we must refer its further development. Even in his day it was but a sentiment. The grossest ignorance still prevailed concerning the practical adaptation of a mediæval spirit to masonry and sculpture. One of the chief merits of the Pointed style is, that the origin of every decorative feature may be traced to a constructive purpose. Thus the stone groining over a cathedral aisle not only presents a vista of graceful curves to the eye of the spectator, but covers the area below it with an almost imperishable roof. The earliest promoters of the

Gothic revival appreciated the superficial effect of such features without recognising the utility which justifies their adoption. Accordingly, the glories of the 'fretted vault' were not unfrequently imitated in lath and plaster; nor were there men of taste wanting to praise the wretched parody.*

Pugin was the first who deftly expounded the true principles of what he not inaptly named Christian art. No man of his day was better fitted to undertake the task. He was by profession an architect. He wrote with considerable ability. He entered on the subject with the full information of an earnest student, and with the zeal of a religious enthusiast. There was, however, one drawback to his efforts. He blended his theological convictions with his theories on art, and the result was that the two became identified in the public mind. He had both causes deeply at heart, but he would have served both better by keeping the subjects distinct. As it was, he sometimes offended the communion he had left by needless allusions to his faith, and sometimes alarmed his fellow-Churchmen by the undue importance which he attached to the style of ecclesiastical decoration. Time has proved that the

* I have entered on this subject more largely in my *History of the Gothic Revival*, published by Messrs. Longman and Co. in 1872.

revival of Gothic architecture is due no more to the teaching of Rome than that of Geneva, and at the present day the pointed arch is almost as much in vogue among Dissenters as it is with Ritualists. The decision of a Parliamentary Commission in 1836—that the new Houses were to be mediæval in character— gave great impetus to the growing taste ; and though the Palace of Westminster may not have realised the highest qualities of the architecture which it is popularly supposed to represent, it has at least proved an excellent school for the encouragement of ancient art. It educated many a sculptor, stonemason, metal-worker, decorator, and cabinet maker, who would otherwise have grown up ignorant of every phase of ornament save that which had reached him by a perverted tradition. Barry, to whose talent are due the merits of the general design, wisely entrusted to Pugin the fashion of those details which were to enrich his structure. Judged by the light of a maturer taste, they may appear deficient in artistic quality. But it is certain that at that time no one could have designed better.

Pugin's active and brilliant career was suddenly interrupted by a melancholy end. But, long before he died, his principles had spread far and wide among the lovers of art—had been adopted and acted on by many of his professional brethren.

In the mind of the general public the spirit of mediæval design is chiefly associated with what has been called 'ecclesiastical sentiment.' But the Gothic revival is not confined to Church architecture. Indeed, if we reflect on the subject, it would seem absurd so to limit its extension. In the best ages of art there was but one style of architecture at one time for every sort of building, whether ecclesiastical or domestic. Some of the best examples of Old English Gothic which exist are certainly either churches or monastic buildings. But at the time they were raised they did not differ in style—they only differed in shape and feature—from the structures by which they were surrounded. If it be urged that dwellings of the fourteenth and fifteenth centuries are not suited to our notions of comfort in regard to arrangement of rooms, light, and ventilation, the answer is, that all these requirements are perfectly compatible with the spirit of ancient art, and that the old designers, as time went on, never hesitated to avail themselves of the march of science, slow as it was in their day.

Mr. Ruskin eloquently described to us the poetry of mediæval art; Pugin and other writers insisted on

its practical advantages. It remained for the rising
generation of architects to profit by the labours of
those able apologists, and to show their patrons that
the prevailing taste had not been called forth by the
whims of a clique or the blind passion of an antiquary,
but that, while based on the sound artistic principles
of early tradition, it might be adapted to the social
habits and requirements of the present age.

That many architects of the present day succeeded
in this effort must be evident to all who have examined
the best examples of domestic architecture which,
under the general name of Gothic, have been erected
within the last twenty years. But artistic taste in the
nineteenth century, based as it is upon eclecticism
rather than on tradition, is capricious and subject to
constant variation. Later influences, which need not
be detailed here, have since diverted the current of
public favour from mediæval art towards those principles of design which prevailed during the seventeenth
and eighteenth centuries, and many an architectural
student who began as an earnest advocate for Gothic
is now a follower of what is commonly called the
' Queen Anne ' school.

Chapter II.

THE ENTRANCE HALL.

HE external aspect of a house, which has not been built expressly for its occupants, is, of course, a question of taste utterly beyond their control. Those who are lucky enough to reside in the picturesque old country mansions which were in vogue long before the nineteenth-century type of cockney villa architecture was introduced, will have no reason to complain; while they whose means have enabled them to combine in their abode the beauty of mediæval design with the necessary comforts and appliances of modern life, may be reckoned still more fortunate. But these are exceptions to the general rule. Most of us are obliged to accept the outward appearance of our abode as we find it. In London it is as a rule irretrievably ugly, and any attempt to alter its character would be met not only by a remonstrance on the part of our landlords, but by an universal objection shared by all of us, and founded upon an inherent disinclination to differ conspicuously from our neighbours. So long as the present system of *tenure* remains as it is, and the interest of house proprietors is to run up buildings which are only required to last a limited number of years, we must remain content with plain brick fronts pierced with the traditional number of square openings, or decorated (in the suburbs) with stucco and cement ornaments, as perishable as they are commonplace and tasteless. Our only license, indeed, is to conceal what we cannot alter. The practice of training ivy and creepers from the basement story to the first-floor, and that of filling the drawing-room balcony with flowering plants, is one which is much increasing at the West-end of London, and it is really the best means by which we can invest our street-fronts, as they are at present designed, with even the smallest degree of interest. The only external feature, therefore, on which it would be worth while to remark, is the front-door. And here, I fear, I must begin to differ from those whose principles of taste are derived from long-accepted conventionalism. The practice of graining wood has not, however, been so long in vogue in this country as to command a traditional respect. It is an objectionable and pretentious deceit, which cannot be excused even on the ground of economy. In the last century, when

English oak and Spanish mahogany could be procured at a reasonable price, the grainer's work was, of
course, unneeded. In modern days the usual substitute for those now expensive woods is deal ; but deal
is so soft and absorbent in its fibre that it becomes
quickly soiled, and in most situations, especially when
exposed to the air, it soon requires painting. But why
should we paint it in imitation of oak ? Everybody
can see at a glance that it is *not* oak, and, as far as
appearance is concerned, there are many modes of
treatment which would be far more effective. For
newly-hung doors in country-houses, the staining fluids
now sold are infinitely preferable, and, when varnish
is superadded, the wood thus protected not only resists
the effects of weather, but reveals its own natural vein,
which is often very pretty. In London we find our
house-doors painted before we take possession, and
therefore we have no choice but to continue painting
them. A good flat tint of olive green or chocolate
colour will, however, answer all practical purposes, and
besides being a more honest and artistic, is really a less
expensive style of decoration.

It is a great pity that the old-fashioned brass
knocker has become obsolete. Though seldom
elegant in form, there was something in its brightness

indicative of a hospitable, well-ordered house. The present cast-iron knocker is a frightful invention ; the only possible fact one can urge in its favour is that it saves work for the housemaid's arm; and gives a little more employment to the footman's. Good *wrought*-iron

knockers, of very fair design and manufacture, may be bought of the many mediæval metal-workers whose branch of art has now become a recognised institution in this country. Ladies are seldom called upon to choose between the merits of wrought and cast-iron for objects of domestic use. But when this is the case, it should be remembered that the work of the hammer and anvil is infinitely superior in every way to the production of the mould. Annexed are two specimens of wrought-iron door-knockers from Wurzburg in Bavaria, dating probably from the close of the sixteenth

century—somewhat too late to exhibit *quite* the right spirit of design. They are conceived and fashioned, however, in thorough accordance with the nature of the material employed, and afford a pleasant contrast to the hackneyed portraits of tame lions and grinning satyrs which have been adopted as types of the modern door-knocker.

In the old towns of Switzerland may frequently be found specimens of highly decorative door-knockers in hammered iron, the design of which dates from the fifteenth and sixteenth centuries. Some examples of these have been reproduced from my drawings by Messrs. Benham and Froud, to whose 'mediæval' metal-work, exemplified in other articles of household use, I shall have occasion to refer in another chapter.

All cast-iron ornament, except under rare conditions,* is bad in style, and when employed to represent wrought work, must be detestable in the eyes of a true artist. Better the simplest form of grate and fender than one loaded with this mean and spiritless system of decoration. Perhaps some of my readers may be curious to know why such an application of this material should be condemned. Although it will not be always possible in this work to enter upon a lengthy justification of opinions which I do not offer on my own authority alone, let me briefly explain, at the outset, a principle universally accepted by those who have made a study of decorative design. Every material used in art manufacture is obviously restricted

---

* The low relief ornament of old Sussex stoves is one of a very few instances in which cast iron has been judiciously applied for decorative purposes.

by the nature of its substance to certain conditions of form. Thus glass, which in a state of fusion can be blown or cut into a thousand fantastic shapes, admirably adapted for drinking-vessels, &c., would, from its brittleness, be utterly unfit for any constructive purpose in which even moderate strength was required. The texture of ordinary free-stone, though capable of being treated with delicacy and refinement by the chisel of a practised sculptor, does not admit of that minute elaboration which we admire in wood-carving. In the manufacture of porcelain, and all kinds of ceramic wares, rotundity is the prominent type of form, while furniture and cabinet-work are generally quadrangular in their main outline ; the general treatment in each case being suggested by the character and properties of the raw material. Whenever this condition is lost sight of, and the material is allowed to assume in design an appearance which is foreign to its own peculiar attributes, the result is invariably inartistic and vulgar. For instance, a glass or plaster column would convey an idea of weakness at once destructive of any sense of beauty which its mere form could excite. A carpet, of which the pattern is shaded in imitation of natural objects, becomes an absurdity when we remember that if it were really what it pretends to be, no one could walk on it with comfort.

If we apply this principle to the treatment of cast-iron, it will be readily perceived that a noble material, which has lost in process of manufacture its most essential quality of strength, can only be further degraded by being invested with forms which feebly imitate not only wrought-iron ornament but stone carving, and even plaster decoration. The simplest argument which can be urged in support of this theory, lies in the fact that while we all appreciate the beauty of such work as the wrought canopy designed by Quentin Matsys for the pump at Antwerp, and the forms of many an old church-door hinge, no one feels the least interest in the cast-iron capitals of a railway-station, or can see aught but black ugliness in a modern kitchen-range. ' And could a kitchen-range ever be otherwise than ugly ?' perhaps some of my readers may be inclined to ask. The fact is, that if the material of which it is composed were properly treated, there is no reason why it should not be as picturesque an object as any in the house. Remember, it is not the humbleness of its purpose or the simplicity of its form which prevents it from being so. How many of us have peeped inside the threshold of a Welsh cottage or Devonshire farmhouse, and longed to sketch its comfortable chimney-corner and ample hearth! Could we say as much for any basement room in Mayfair? And yet there was a time when no such difference existed between the appointments of town and country dwellings.

Let us then quietly enter one of these respectable, luxurious, but eminently uninteresting London mansions, and try to discover what there is about their internal arrangement which makes them such hopeless subjects for the artist's pencil. The first thing on which our foot rests is a useful article of household furniture with the style of which no one can find fault— the street-door mat. In common with most objects of its class which for many generations past have been made in the country, it fulfils its purpose in every way without pretending to that false 'elegance' of design, which we shall probably detect upstairs in the silly lumps of blue or mauve-stained wool, called drawing-room door-rugs. What people want to rub their shoes upon is a strong rough material, such as we find in the hall or at the foot of the principal staircase. To preserve the fiction of this necessity throughout the rest of the house is a mistake, but to manufacture a false sheepskin, and dye it of so delicate a colour that we are afraid even to step upon it for the purpose of wiping our boots, becomes absurd.

There can be little doubt that the best mode of treating a hall-floor, whether in town or country, is to pave it with encaustic tiles. This branch of art-manufacture is one of the most hopeful, in regard to taste, now carried on in this country. It has not only reached great technical perfection as far as material and colour are concerned, but, aided by the designs supplied by many architects of acknowledged skill, it has gradually become a means of decoration which, for beauty of effect, durability, and cheapness, has scarcely a parallel. To Messrs. Minton, I believe, we are indebted for the earliest revival of this ancient art in modern times. The tiles manufactured by Mr. W. Godwin have long been noted for the artistic quality of their colour and design. But for rich variety of pattern, and for the skill with which the best types of ornament have been adapted for enamelled ware, plain tile pavements, mosaic and mural decoration, the ware produced by Messrs. Maw & Co., of Salop, stands almost unrivalled. A few specimens of their pavements and tile borders, especially fitted for household use, have been selected for illustration here, from the very numerous examples published by that firm.

V

Encaustic Tile Pavements.

Manufactured by Messrs. Maw and Co.

Hall Pavements.
Manufactured by Messrs. Maw and Co.

Pavement and Tile Borders.
Manufactured by Messrs. Maw and Co.

VIII

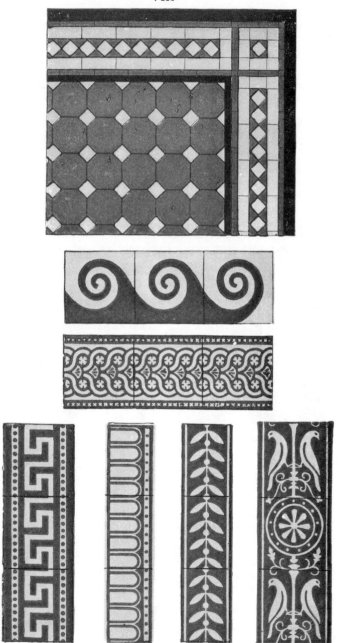

Pavement and Tile Borders.
Manufactured by Messrs. Maw and Co.

When the material known as 'floor-cloth' was first used in this country for halls and passages, its design began with an imitation of marble pavements and parquetry floors, I have even seen a pattern which was intended to represent the spots on a leopard's skin. These conceits were thoroughly false in principle, and are now being gradually abandoned. A floor-cloth, like every other article of manufacture to which design can be implied, should seem to be what it really is, and not affect the appearance of a richer material. There are endless varieties of geometrical diaper which could be used for floor-cloth, without resorting to the foolish expedient of copying the knots and veins of wood and marble. Some very fair examples of such geometrical patterns may occasionally be met with, but, as a rule, too many colours are introduced in them. However attractive it may appear in the shop, this kind of polychromy ought studiously to be avoided on the floor of a private house. Two tints, or — better still — two shades of the same tint (which should not be a *positive* colour) will be found most suitable for the purpose, and in any case there should be no attempt to indicate relief or raised ornament in the pattern.

The mural decoration of the hall is a point con-

cerning which modern conventionalism and true principles of design are sure to clash.   There can be
little doubt that the most agreeable wall-lining which
could be devised for such a place is marble, and next
to that *real* wainscoting.   In former days, when wood
was cheaper than it is now, oak panels were commonly
used, not only in the halls and passages, but in many
rooms of even a small-sized London house.   At the
present time, when both marble and oak are beyond
the reach of ordinary incomes, the usual practice is to
cover the walls with a paper stained and varnished in
imitation of marble.   This is, perhaps, a more excus-
able sham than others to which I have alluded ; but still
it *is* a sham, and ought therefore to be condemned.   Of
course, when people find themselves in a house where
such an expedient has been already adopted, any
alteration in this respect would involve considerable
expense.   But in cases where the difficulty may be
anticipated, it is as well to remember that modern
manufacture, or rather the revival of an ancient art,
has supplied an admirable substitute for marble veneering at a comparatively low price.   An inlay of encaustic
tiles, to a height, say, of three or four feet from the
ground, would form an excellent lining for a hall
or ground-floor passage.   Above that level the wall

IX.

Mural Decoration (for a 'Dado')

executed by Messrs. Heaton, Butler, & Bayne.

HANCOCK, ELECTRO-PHOTO

might either be painted in the usual manner, or the plaster washed with flatted colour. The latter is certainly more liable to be soiled than oil-paint, but is far pleasanter in effect, and at a level of four feet from the floor-line would be safely removed from contact with ladies' dresses and the chance of careless finger-marks.

A cheaper and, in good hands, a very effective mode of wall-decoration for a hall is by distemper-painting. The example here given is from a sketch by Mr. C. Heaton (of the firm of Heaton, Butler & Bayne), whose excellent taste in the design of stained-glass windows and mural decoration is well known.

The colour of the walls must necessarily depend on circumstances, the amount of light admitted being the first consideration. In cases where, as is too often the case, a small fanlight over the entrance-door is all the provision made for illumining the hall, it will be as well to choose a delicate green or warm grey tint. Where, on the contrary, there is plenty of light, the dull red hue, which may still be traced on the walls of Pompeii, and on the relics of ancient Egypt, will be found an excellent surface colour.

Before discussing the subject of the hall furniture, it will be as well to say something on the subject of furniture in general.

Not many years ago there was scarcely an uphol
sterer in London at whose establishment good artistic
furniture of modern date and moderate price was kept
in stock for sale. For years past this branch of art-
manufacture had been entrusted to those whose taste,
if it may be called taste at all, could be no more referred to correct principles of design than the gimcrack
decorations of a wedding-cake could be tested by any
standard of sculpturesque beauty. It may be urged, in
answer to this parallel, that in the latter case it would
be superfluous to apply such a test. Without even
admitting this to be so (for in the best ages of art the
commonest article of household use, down to the very
door-nails, had an appropriate form of beauty of its
own), it is obvious that, although we may tolerate in-
sipid prettiness in perishable confectionary, we ought
not to do so in objects which become associated with
our daily life, and which are so eminently characteristic
of our national habits. There are few persons of education and refinement who do not feel interested in architecture, but I would ask, of what use is it to decorate
the exterior of our country-houses if we are to permit
ugliness within them?—and ugliness we shall be sure
to have if the choice of furniture is left to ordinary
upholsterers. Indeed, their notions of the beautiful

are either centred in mere novelty, or derived from
traditions of the Louis Quatorze period. That school
of decorative art, bad and vicious in principle as it
was, had a certain air of luxury and grandeur about it
which was due to elaboration of detail and richness of
material. Its worst characteristic was an extravagance
of *contour*, and this is just the only characteristic which
the tradition of upholstery preserved. The sofas and
chairs of the last generation laid claim to elegance, not
for their gaily embossed silk or delicate inlay of wood,
but simply because there was not a straight line in
their composition. Now a curve, especially of such a
kind as cannot be drawn by artificial means, is a beautiful feature when rightly applied to decorative art,
whether we find it as the appendage to an old Missal
letter, or bounding the *entasis* of a Greek column.
But a curve at the back of a sofa means nothing at all,
and is manifestly inconvenient, for it must render it
either too high in one place or too low in another to
accommodate the shoulders of a sitter. The tendency
of the last age of upholstery was to run into curves.
Chairs were invariably curved in such a manner as to
ensure the greatest amount of ugliness with the least
possible comfort. The backs of sideboards were
curved in the most senseless and extravagant manner ;

the legs of cabinets were curved, and became in consequence constructively weak ; drawing-room tables were curved in every direction—perpendicularly and horizontally—and were therefore inconvenient to sit at, and always rickety.   In marble wash-stands the useful shelf, which should run the whole length of the rear, was frequently omitted in order to ensure a curve. This detestable system of ornamentation was called 'shaping.' It always involves additional expense in manufacture, and therefore by avoiding 'shaped' articles of furniture, the public will not only discourage a bad style of art, but may also save their pockets.

I am only now treating of furniture in general terms ; but under this head may be discussed two important points connected with its ordinary manufacture, viz., veneering and carved work.   The former has been so long in vogue, and is apparently so cheap and easy a means of obtaining a valuable result, that it is always difficult to persuade people of its inexpedience.   Veneering has been condemned by some writers on the same grounds on which false jewellery should (of course) be condemned.   But the two cases are scarcely analogous.   If we are to tolerate the marble lining of a brick wall and the practice of silver-plating goods of baser metal—now too universally recognised to be considered in the light of a deception—I do not see exactly how veneering is to be rejected on 'moral' grounds. The nature of walnut-wood prevents it from being used, except at a great expense, in any other way than as a veneer; and when, for instance, in piano cases, the leaves are so disposed as to reverse their grain symmetrically, after the manner of the marble 'wall veils' of St. Mark's at Venice, the arrangement is not only very beautiful in effect, but at once proclaims the means by which that effect is attained.

There are, however, many practical objections to the mode of veneering in present use. To cover inferior wood completely in this fashion, thin and fragile joints must be used, which every cabinetmaker knows are incompatible with perfect construction. The veneer itself is far too slight in substance, and, even when laid down with the utmost nicety, is liable to blister, especially when used for washing-stands, or in any situation where it is exposed to accidental damp. It is never worth while to buy furniture veneered with mahogany, for a little additional cost may procure the same articles in solid wood. Not long ago I had a substantial oak table made from my own design at a price which was much less than what I should have paid for one veneered with rosewood or walnut.

The most legitimate mode of employing veneer would be in panels not less than a quarter of an inch in thickness, and, if used for horizontal surfaces, the inferior wood should be allowed to retain a border of its own in the solid. By this means no thin edges would be exposed to injury, and the design might be treated in an honest and straightforward manner.

The subject of carved work is a more important question, because nothing but a vigorous and radical reform will help us on this point. It may be laid down as a general rule, that wherever wood-carving is introduced in the design of second-rate furniture it is egregiously and utterly bad. It is frequently employed in the most inappropriate places—it is generally spiritless in design, and always worthless in execution. The wood-carver may indeed be an artist, but the ordinary furniture-carver has long since degenerated into a machine. The fact is that a great deal of his work is literally done by machinery. There are shops where enriched wood-mouldings may be bought by the yard, leaf-brackets by the dozen, and ' scroll-work,' no doubt, by the pound. I use the word ' scroll-work ' in its common acceptation to denote that indescribable species of ornament which may be seen round drawing-room mirrors and the gilded consoles of a pier-glass. It is not easy to say whence this extraordinary type of decoration first arose. The most charitable supposition is that, in its origin, it was intended for conventionalised foliage ; in its present state it resembles a conglomeration of capital G's. Even if it were carved out of the solid wood, it would be very objectionable in design; but this trash is only lightly *glued* to the frame which it is supposed to adorn, and may indeed frequently be removed with infinite advantage to the general effect. The carving introduced in other articles of furniture is, as a rule, of a very meagre description. In fact, under existing circumstances, and until we can get good work of this kind, it would be far better to omit it altogether.

It is lamentable to notice also how much the turner's art has degenerated. Even down to the middle of the last century it was employed with great advantage in the manufacture of chairs, tables, banister-rails, &c. The judicious association of the ' bead, fillet, and hollow' for mouldings was a simple, honest, and frequently effective mode of decoration. It still lingers in some of the minor articles of household use which have been allowed to escape the innovations of modern taste. Among these may be mentioned the common ' Windsor' chair and the bed-room towel-horse. A careful examination of these humble specimens of home manufacture will show that they are really superior in point of design to many pretentious elegan-

cies of fashionable make. Indeed, it will generally be found, that the most commonplace objects of domestic use, in England as well as on the Continent, are the most interesting in appearance. We have at the pre-

sent time no more artistic workman in his way than
the country cartwright. His system of construction is
always sound, and such little decoration as he is
enabled to introduce never seems inappropriate,
because it is in accordance with the traditional development of original and necessary forms.

It is to be feared that the decline of our national
taste must be attributed to a cause which is popularly
supposed to have encouraged a contrary effect, viz.,
competition. It is a general complaint with those who
have the employment of art-workmen, that, while a
higher price is paid for their labour, its result is not
nearly so satisfactory as it was before the Great
Exhibition of 1851. That, however, is a point on
which it would be beside my present purpose to enter.
But it is very certain that, if our ordinary furniture has
cheapened in price, it has also deteriorated in quality,
while the best furniture has become extravagantly
dear. Some years ago I visited the establishment of
an upholsterer, who announced that to meet the
requirements of the public he had taken up the *spécialité* of mediæval art. I inquired whether he had any
drawing-room chairs in that style, and was shown some
examples—rich in material, but very simple in construction. I inquired the price, and found it was no

less than six guineas! Their prime cost must have
been about 2*l.* 10*s.* It would be absurd to suppose
that while such profits as this are demanded for every
article of furniture which does not partake of the
stereotyped form in use, we can ever hope for a revival of good manufacture. Anyone can get drawing-
room chairs designed by an architect and executed by
private contract for six guineas per chair. What the
public required was a shop where such articles were
kept in stock and could be purchased for half that sum.

In attempting a solution of this difficulty, the old
question of 'demand and supply' was once more raised.
The upholsterers declared themselves willing to give
more attention to the subject of design as soon as the
nature of public taste became defined. The public,
on the other hand, complained that they could only
choose from what they saw in the shops. It is not improbable that there was a little apathy on both sides,
but it was necessary that one should take the lead,
and it is certain that at the present time when well-
designed and artistic furniture is offered for sale at a
reasonable price, and under proper management, there
is no difficulty in finding purchasers.*

---

* Among the various firms which have lately given attention to this
subject, I may mention Messrs. Jackson and Graham, several specimens
of whose cabinet work are illustrated in this volume.

There is no portion of a modern house which indicates more respect for the early traditions of art, as
applied to furniture, than the Entrance-hall. The
dining-room may have yielded to the influence of
fashion in its upholstery ; the drawing-room may be
crowded with silly knick-knacks, crazy chairs and
tables, and all those shapeless extravagances which
passed for elegance in the last generation ; the bed-
rooms may depend for their decoration on the taste of
a man-milliner ; but the fittings of the hall at least assume an appearance of solidity which is characteristic
of a better aim in design. No doubt this peculiarity
is mainly due to the fact that, being only used as a
means of communication between the street and the
habitable portion of a house, it is not thought necessary
that its furniture should be of that light and easily
moveable description which is deemed requisite elsewhere. And here it will be well to note two facts
connected with this point : first, that although it may
be desirable to make drawing-room chairs and tables
conveniently light, it is no convenience to find them
so light as to be fragile, rickety, and easily upset ;
secondly, that there is no reasonable condition of
modern convenience with which true principles of
design are not compatible.

The hall-table is generally made of oak, in a plain and substantial manner, flanked by chairs of the same material, with a hat and umbrella-stand to correspond. Sometimes a bench is substituted for the chairs, but in any case this group of furniture is generally the best in the house, on account of its extreme simplicity.

The design given in the annexed woodcut shows how the ordinary type of hall-table for small houses may be varied without increase of cost, at least to any appreciable extent, and supposing each article to be of sound workmanship and material.

I would especially caution my readers against the contemptible specimens of that pseudo-Gothic joinery which is manufactured in the back-shops of Soho. No doubt good examples of mediæval furniture and cabinet-work are occasionally to be met with in the curiosity shops of Wardour Street; but, as a rule, the 'Glastonbury' chairs and 'antique' book-cases sold in that venerable thoroughfare will prove on examination to be nothing but gross libels on the style of art which they are supposed to represent. A fragment of Jacobean woodcarving, or a single 'linen-fold' panel, is frequently considered a sufficient authority for the construction of a massive sideboard, which bears no more relation to the genuine work of the Middle Ages than the diaphanous paper of recent invention does to the stained-glass of our old cathedrals. In other words, these elaborate fittings for the hall and library are forgeries,

made up of odds and ends grafted on modern carpentry of a weak and paltry description. Not only is the rudeness of old carving parodied, without an atom of its real spirit, but the very construction of the articles

in question is defective. Nails and screws are substituted for the stout wooden pins and tenon-joints
used in mediæval framing; mouldings, instead of
being worked in the solid wood, are ' run ' in separate
strips, and only *glued* into their places; cracks and fissures are filled up with putty, and the whole surface is
often smeared thickly over with a dark varnish, partly
to conceal these flaws, and partly to give that appearance of age which the mere *virtuoso* will always regard
with interest.

Now, though the age of old woodwork does, indeed,
enhance the beauty of its colour, that is by no means
its highest recommendation. The real secret of its
value lies in the immense superiority of ancient over
modern workmanship, both as regards joinery and
decorative carving. For many years the former art so
declined that it was extremely difficult, if not impossible—except, perhaps, in some remote provincial town
—to meet with a specimen of thoroughly good work
exposed for ordinary sale. At the present time, when
direct supervision is exercised by a qualified designer,
and in the class of furniture which is called 'artistic,'
more attention is given to this branch, and the result
is very different; but the goods kept in stock at your
ordinary upholsterer's, however showy in appearance,

Hall Chair at Cothele, Devon,
in the possession of the Earl of Mount Edgcumbe.

are still, in nine cases out of ten, put together on completely false principles of construction. The best proof of this is, that whereas an old oaken chair or table made a century or two ago will frequently be found in excellent condition at the present day, much of our modern furniture becomes rickety in a few years, and rarely, if ever, survives a lifetime.

The sketch of a hall-chair which appears as an illustration to this chapter is taken from one in the possession of the Earl of Mount-Edgcumbe at Cothele, a charming old Tudor mansion on the Cornish side of the River Tamar, where there are many excellent and interesting specimens of ancient English furniture.

As for carving, its degeneracy is the more to be lamented, because there never was an age when the hand of the artisan was more apt, or his tools more excellent, than at the present time. There are hundreds of Englishmen now following this trade who will imitate in wood, with astonishing precision and delicacy, the feathered forms of dead game, or reproduce, line for line and leaf for leaf, a festoon of real flowers. I am sorry to tell those of my fair readers who have not turned their attention to these matters that the carver's skill is utterly wasted on such work. It is an estab-

lished principle in the theory of design, that decorative
art is degraded when it passes into a direct imitation of
natural objects. Young ladies who may find this difficult to understand, should remember that they recognise the selfsame principle in a hundred different ways
on matters of ordinary and even conventional taste.
You admire the roses and azaleas which the most
skilful flower-painter of our day—Miss Mutrie—groups
together for a picture subject, but what would you say
to see them transferred as a pattern to the skirt of
your dress, or even to the tablecloth of your boudoir ?
Well, then, precisely as your good taste shows you
that a naturally shaded and coloured representation of
flowers would be out of place on silk or damask, so you
may conceive that to an educated eye a literal reproduction in wood or stone of the actual forms assumed
by animal or vegetable life is by no means agreeable.
The truth is that, under such circumstances, nature may
be typified or symbolised, but not actually imitated.
The beauty of Indian shawls, and indeed of all Oriental objects of textile fabric, is too universally admitted
to need any comment in these pages. Did you ever
see any *picture* of bird, beast, or flower on these specimens of Eastern manufacture ? Would you not at
once set down as vulgar and commonplace any attempt

in this direction, whether for articles of dress or *tapis-serie ?* Renounce them henceforth, and for analogous reasons, those trophies of slaughtered hares and partridges which you may occasionally see standing out in bold relief from the backboard of a buffet or the door of a cabinet. Many of them are cleverly executed it is true, but they are in a bad and vicious style of art. Wood-carving applied as a means of decoration in such places should be treated after a thoroughly *abstract* fashion, and made subservient to the general design of the furniture. If you desire an example of this mode of treatment, examine the choir-stalls of the next cathedral which you visit, and do not suppose that the sacred nature of the edifice influenced in the least degree the character of the carved work. If you were to light upon an old 'armoire' or buttery-safe of the same period, you would find precisely the same *spirit* of design, although the design itself might be of a different character. Many people suppose that Gothic architecture means ecclesiastical architecture, simply because the best specimens of that style are to be found in old churches and conventual buildings. But though in the Middle Ages there was but one sort of architecture at a time, no one ever thought of giving an ordinary domestic house the appearance of a church, or of allowing a church to appear like anything but what it was. Each structure at once proclaimed its object —not by a difference of style, but by a certain fitness of arrangement which it was impossible to mistake. We fall into the double error of adopting endless varieties of style at one time, and yet allowing buildings raised for totally opposite purposes to resemble each other in form. The same fallacy is repeated throughout the whole system of British manufacture. We copy the bronzes of France, the mosaics of Italy, the pottery of China, the carpets of Turkey, with indifferent success; and, not content with this jumble, we invent objects constructed of one material with the form and ornamental character which should be the attributes of another. By this means decorative art has been degraded in this country to a level from which it is only now beginning to rise.

Chapter III.

THE DINING-ROOM.

AMONG the many fallacies engendered in the mind of the modern upholsterer, and delivered by him as wholesome doctrine to a credulous public, was the notion that all conditions of decorative art must necessarily vary with the situation in which that art is employed. It was not sufficient for him to tell us that the dining-room table and sideboard should, on account of the use to which they are put, be made after a more solid fashion than the drawing-room table and the cheffonier. Not content with informing his customers (if, indeed, they need such information) that book-cases would be required for the library, and that flower-stands are suitable for the boudoir, he proceeded with great gravity to lay down a series of rules by which certain types of form and certain shades of colour were to be, for some mysterious reason best known to himself, for ever associated with certain apartments in the house. In obedience to this injunction, people whose taste is guided by mere custom sit down to dine upon an oaken chair before an oaken table, with a turkey carpet under their feet, and a red flock-paper staring them in the face. After dinner the ladies ascend into a green-and-gold-papered drawing-room, to perform on a walnut-wood piano, having first seated themselves on walnut-wood music-stools, while their friends are reclining on a walnut-wood sofa, protected from the heat of the fire by a walnut-wood screen. A few years ago, all these last-mentioned articles of household furniture were made of rosewood. In the early part of this century it was *de rigueur* that they should be mahogany ; so the fashion of taste goes on changing from age to age; and I firmly believe that, if Society prescribed that staircases should be hung with *moire antique,* and that the drawing-room fender ought in summer time to be planted with mignonette, there are people who would repose implicit confidence in such opinions.

Take, for instance, the case of carpets. If the chaste and deftly associated colours which characterize the Oriental loom are right, and content us downstairs, why should we lapse into the vulgarity of garlands and bouquets for the decoration of our drawing-room floors ? And so with regard to cabinet-work. It is of course unnecessary to fit up a boudoir with furniture of the size and capacity which we require in a dining-room sideboard. But though the shape of a cheffonier may differ from that of a buffet, there can be no reason whatever why the *style of design* in these respective articles of furniture should vary. We may require, in a modern reception-room, chairs of a lighter make and more easily moveable than those in a library, but why the former should necessarily have round seats and the latter square ones is a mystery which no one but an upholsterer could explain.

The truth is, there used to be an absurd conventionality about such points as these, to which most of us submitted under a vague impression that if we differed from our neighbours we should be violating good taste. We passed from one principle of design for the ground-floor, to another completely distinct one when we had ascended two flights of stairs. We left a solid, gloomy, and often cumbersome class of furniture below, to find a flimsy and extravagant one above. It may be a question which of these two extremes is the more objectionable. Judged by the standard of any recognised principles in art-manufacture, they would probably both be considered wrong. But it is obvious that they cannot both be right.

In the early part of the present century a fashionable conceit prevailed of fitting up separate apartments in large mansions each after a style of its own. Thus we had Gothic halls, Elizabethan chambers, Louis Quatorze drawing-rooms, &c., &c., all under one roof. It is scarcely possible to imagine any system of housefurnishing more absurd and mischievous in its effect upon uneducated taste than this. Indeed, it was the practical evidence that a healthy and genuine taste was altogether wanting. Choose what style of furniture we may, it should surely be adopted throughout the house we live in.

Among the dining-room appointments, the table is an article of furniture which still stands greatly in need of reform. It is generally made of planks of polished oak or mahogany laid upon an insecure framework of the same material, and supported by four gouty legs, ornamented by the turner with mouldings which look like inverted cups and saucers piled upon an attic baluster. I call the framework insecure because I am describing what is commonly called a 'telescope' table, or one which can be pulled out to twice its usual length, and, by the addition of extra leaves in its middle, accommodates twice the usual number of diners. Such a table cannot be soundly made in the same sense that ordinary furniture is sound. It must depend for its support on some contrivance which is not consistent with the material of which it is made. Few people would like to sit on a chair the legs of

which were made to slide in and out, and were fastened at the required height with a pin. There would be a sense of insecurity in the notion eminently unpleasant. You might put up with such an invention in camp, or on a sketching expedition, but to have it and use it under your own roof, instead of a strong and service-

able chair, would be absurd. Yet this is very much
what we do in the case of the modern dining-room
table. When it is extended it looks weak and untidy
at the sides ; when it is reduced to its shortest length,
the legs appear heavy and ill-proportioned. It is
always liable to get out of order, and from the very
nature of its construction must be an inartistic object.
Why should such a table be made at all ? A dining-
room is a room to dine in. Whether there are few or
many people seated for that purpose, the table might
well be kept of an uniform length ; and if space is an
object, it is always possible to use in its stead two
small tables, one of them being fitted with 'flap'
leaves, but each on four legs. These tables might be
placed end to end when dinner-parties are given, and
one of them would suffice for family use, while the
other with its 'flap' leaves folded down might stand
against the wall or be used elsewhere. Tables of this
kind might be solidly and stoutly framed, so as to last
for ages, and become, as all furniture ought to become,
an heirloom in the family. When a man builds himself
a house on freehold land, he does not intend that it
shall only last his lifetime ; he bequeaths it in sound
condition to posterity. We ought to be ashamed of
furniture which is continually being replaced. At all

events, we cannot possibly take any interest in such furniture. In former days, when the principles of good joinery were really understood, the legs of such a large table as that of the dining-room would have been made of a very different form from the lumpy pear-shaped things of modern use.

The annexed woodcut is from a sketch of a table in the possession of Mr. E. Corbauld, dating probably from the Jacobean period. It is of a very simple but picturesque design, and is certainly sound in principle of construction. Observe how cleverly the mouldings are distributed in the legs to give variety of outline without weakening them. In the modern 'telescope table,' on the contrary, the mouldings are extravagant in contour, and the diameter of the legs is thereby reduced in some places to much less than the width necessary for strength. The whole ingenuity of the modern joiner has been concentrated on a clumsy attempt to make his table serve two purposes, viz., for large or small dinner-parties ; but the old joiner has shown his skill in decorating his table-frame with a delicate bas-relief of ornament. And remember that it was from no lack of skill that this old table was not made capable of being enlarged at pleasure. The social customs of the age in which it was produced did not require such a piece of mechanism. In those days the dining-table was of one uniform length whether a few or many guests were assembled at it; and of the two fashions the ancient one certainly seems to indicate a more frequent and open hospitality. But be

that as it may, if the Jacobean table had been required for occasional extension, we may be certain it would have been so constructed, and that too on a more workmanlike principle than our foolish telescope slide. In like manner, if the ladies and gentlemen of King James's time had found (as probably those of Queen

Victoria's time would find) the wooden rail which runs
from end to end of the table inconvenient for their
feet, it would assuredly have been omitted. As it
was, they probably kept their feet on the other side of

it, or used it as a footstool. But to show how both
these modern requirements may be met without
forsaking the spirit of ancient work, I give a sketch of
a modern table constructed in accordance with old
principles of design, but in such a manner that it may

be lengthened for occasional use at each end, while
the framing is arranged so that any one may sit at it
with perfect convenience.   In this case the additional
'leaves' are supported by wooden bearers which run

parallel with the sides of the table, and may be pulled
out by means of little rings attached to their ends.

In this example, as in that of the Jacobean table,
sunk castors could easily be introduced in the foot of
each leg; but such an appliance is by no means
necessary or desirable.   A dining-table rarely requires

to be moved from its ordinary position. It should stand firmly on its legs at each corner. When it is fitted with castors, servants are perpetually pushing it awry.

The other tables represented are portions of the ancient furniture contained in the Rathhaus at Ochsen-

furth, near Wurzburg, in Bavaria. They are made of pine, and constructed in such a manner that they can be taken to pieces with the greatest ease when occasion requires. The building which contains these and many other curious examples of mediæval furniture was completed in the year 1499, and probably the tables date from the same period, when it was customary to sit at only one side of the dining-table, while servants waited at the other. For this reason the tables are narrow, and do not afford accommodation for sitters at each end. With a little alteration they might, however, be easily adapted for modern use, and in any case they may serve as good examples of a design which is not only picturesque in effect, but practical and workmanlike as far as construction is concerned.

Without both these qualities all furniture is, in an artistic sense, worthless. And they are precisely the qualities which, until lately, were disregarded in modern manufacture. Examine the framing of a fashionable sofa made say ten years ago, and you will find it was put together in such a manner as to conceal as far as possible the principle of its strength. Ask any artist of taste whether there is a single object in an ordinary upholsterer's shop that he would care to paint as a study of 'still life,' and he would tell you, not one. We must not infer from this that such objects are unpaintable simply because they are *new*. A few years' wear will soon fade silk or damask down to what might be a pleasant gradation of tint if the material be originally of a good and noble colour. A few years' use would soon invest our chairs and tables with that sort of interest which age alone can give, if their designs were originally artistic. But, unfortunately, most of our modern furniture does not become picturesque with time—it only grows shabby. The ladies like it best when it comes like a new toy from the shop, fresh with recent varnish and untarnished gilding. And they are right; for in this transient prettiness rests the single merit which it possesses.

The annexed woodcut represents a sofa suitable for a dining-room, and really far more comfortable than one with a 'shaped' back and sides. It may be made either in oak or walnut, and covered with figured velvet or one of the many artistically designed textile fabrics which are now manufactured.

Some years ago, when our chairs and tables were 'hand-polished,' the English house-wife took a certain pride in their sheen, which was produced by a vast amount of manual labour on the part of footmen or housemaids. The present system of French-polishing, or literally *varnishing*, furniture is destructive of all artistic effect in its appearance, because the surface of wood thus lacquered can never change its colour, or acquire that rich hue which is one of the chief charms of old cabinet-work.

To return, however, to the question of design ; it is obvious that whatever reform is attempted in the field of household taste should be in strict conformity with modern requirements, to ignore which would be sheer affectation.

The general arrangement of an ordinary English sideboard is reasonable enough. It consists of a wide and deep shelf fitted with one or two drawers, and resting at each end on a cellaret cupboard. If this piece of furniture were constructed in a plain and straightforward manner, and were additionally provided with a few narrow shelves at the rear for displaying the old china vases and rare porcelain, of which almost every house contains a few examples, what a picturesque appearance it might present at the end of a room ! Instead of this, fashion once more stepped in and twisted the unfortunate buffet into all sorts of indescribable curves. It was bowed in front and 'shaped' at the back : the cupboard doors were bent inwards ; the drawer-fronts were bent outwards ; the angles were rounded off ; tasteless mouldings were glued on ; the whole surface glistened with varnish, and the result was—eminently uninteresting.

Dining-room Sideboard,
executed from a design by Charles L. Eastlake.

To fulfil the first and most essential principles of good design, every article of furniture should, at the first glance, proclaim its real purpose ; but the second-rate upholsterers seem to think it betokens elegance when that purpose is concealed. Having already touched on the subject of wood-carving, as applied to the decoration of such objects, I will only add that, whatever the faults of its modern treatment may be, they are rendered doubly objectionable by the application of varnish. The moment a carved or sculptured surface begins to *shine*, it loses interest. But machine-made ornament, invested with an artificial lustre, is an artistic enormity which should be universally discouraged.

I know no better examples of dining-room chairs than some made in the early part of the seventeenth century which still exist in excellent preservation at Knole (near Sevenoaks), the seat of the late Earl De La Warr, to whose courtesy I am indebted for permission to make several of the sketches which illustrate these pages. If any of my readers wish to see furniture designed upon thoroughly artistic principles, they should visit this interesting old mansion, where they may walk through room after room and gallery after gallery filled with choice and rich specimens of ancient furniture, most of which has remained intact since the reign of James I.* I had the good fortune myself to discover a slip of paper tucked beneath the webbing of a settee there, and bearing an inscription in Old

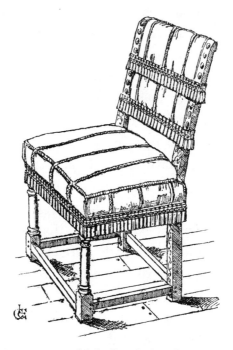

English characters which fixed the date of some of this furniture indubitably at 1620. The sofas and chairs of that period are constructed of a light-coloured close-grained wood, the rails and legs being properly pinned

* Knole House is now, unfortunately, closed to the public.

together and painted, where the framework is visible,
with a red lacquer which is ornamented with a delicate

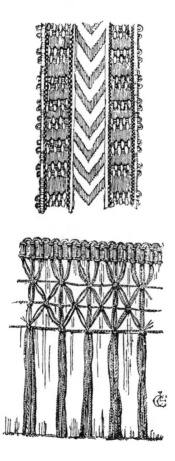

foliated pattern in gold. The stuff with which they
are covered was originally a rose-coloured velvet,

which has now faded into a scarcely less beautiful
silver-grey. The backs and seats are divided into

panels by a trimming composed of silk and gold
thread woven into a pattern of excellent design, and

are also decorated horizontally with a knotted fringe of the same material. The armchairs of the same set are of two kinds—one constructed with columnar legs like the smaller chair; the others framed after a more picturesque fashion, but painted in the same style. The side-rails which support the back are studded, over the velvet, with large round copper-gilt nails punched with a geometrical pattern, while a larger quatrefoil-headed nail marks the intersection of the framed legs below. The back consists of three rails, one at each side and one at the top, the lower rail being, evidently for comfort's sake, omitted. Between these three rails a stout canvas bag is stretched, stuffed like the seat—which retains its elasticity to this day— with down or feathers, but to scarcely a greater thick- ness than an inch. Thus, without assuming the pad- ded lumpy appearance of a modern armchair, the back so constructed accommodates

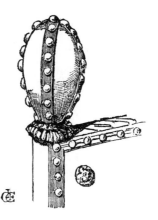

itself at once to the shoulders of the sitter, and forms a most luxurious support. The egg-shaped finials at each angle of the back are composed of wood whipped over with thread silk, and decorated with gold braid and gilt nails.

I give a full description of this chair because I consider it one of the most sumptuous examples of its class which I have ever seen. The costliness of its material and mode of decoration may indeed render it unlikely that such furniture will ever be revived for ordinary use in our own day. But the general principle of the design need involve no more expense in execution than the best specimens of modern upholstery.

There has been a slight improvement of late in the design of modern dining-room chairs, but they are still very far from what they ought to be ; and the best are rather expensive. Perhaps the most satisfactory type is that which is commonly known in the trade as the 'Cromwell' chair. Its form is evidently copied from examples of the seventeenth century. The seat is square, or nearly so, in plan ; the legs are partly square and partly turned ; the back slopes slightly outwards and presents a padded frame, stretched between two upright rails, to the shoulders of the sitter. Both the seat and shoulder-pad are stuffed, or supposed to be stuffed, with horsehair, and are covered with leather,

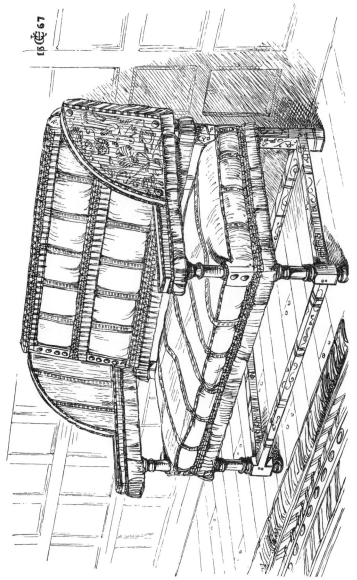

XII.

Settee in Billiard Room at Knole.

Date, 1620.

studded round the edge with brass nails. Messrs. Jackson and Graham have recently executed some chairs of this description (with armchairs to match) the design being adapted from an Old English model of a simple and inexpensive type.

A feeling is, I trust, being gradually awakened in favour of 'art furniture.' But the universal obstacle to its popularity up to the present time has been the cost which it entails on people of ordinary means. And this is a very natural obstacle. It would be quixotic to expect any one but a wealthy enthusiast to pay twice as much as his neighbour for chairs and tables in the cause of art. The true principles of good design are universally applicable, and, if they are worth anything, can be brought to bear on all sorts and conditions of manufacture. There was a time when this was so ; and, indeed, it is certain that they lingered in the cottage long after they had been forgotten in palaces.

Every article of manufacture which is capable of decorative treatment should indicate, by its general design, the purpose to which it will be applied, and should never be allowed to convey a false notion of that purpose. Experience has shown that particular shapes and special modes of decoration are best suited

to certain materials. Therefore the character, situation,
and extent of ornament should depend on the nature
of the material employed, as well as on the use of the
article itself. On the acceptance of these two leading
principles—now universally recognised in the field of
decorative art—must always depend the chief merit of
good design. To the partial, and often direct, violation of those principles, we may attribute the vulgarity
and bad taste of most modern work.

Let us take a familiar example of household furniture by way of illustration. A coal-box, or scuttle, is
intended to contain a very useful, but dirty, species of
fuel. It is evident, looking to the weight of the substance which it is destined to hold, that iron or brass
must be the best and most suitable material of which a
coal-box could be made. It is also obvious that, if it
be invested with any ornamental character beyond
that which may be afforded by its general form, such
ornament should be of the simplest description, executed in colour of the soberest hues. But what is the
usual coal-box of our day ? Brass has been almost
entirely discarded in its manufacture, and though iron
is retained, it is lacquered over with delicate tints, and
patterns of flowers, &c., utterly unsuitable in such a
place. Nor is this all. Of late years *photographs*

have been introduced as an appropriate decoration for the lid and sides. Could absurdity of design be carried farther ? We might, with as much artistic propriety, make *papier-mâché* flower-pots, and hang our chimney-pieces with point-lace.

Almost all the quondam 'fashionable' shapes for fenders, grates, and fire-irons, were selected on a prin-ciple which utterly ignored the material of which they were made. The old type of fender in use about sixty years ago consisted of thin iron plates, perforated and framed between bars of brass or steel. It was often graceful in design, and infinitely better art than the curvilinear and elaborate monstrosities which are pro-duced in Birmingham and Sheffield at the present time. Moreover, it answered the purpose of protecting women's dress from contact with the fire much more effectually than the flat fenders in cast iron and ormolu.

I am glad to find that many ironmongers are now reproducing these old patterns at a reasonable price. In this and a hundred other cases the taste of the public and of the manufacturers became vitiated from a false notion of what constitutes beauty of form. Every article of upholstery which has a curved outline, no matter of what kind the curve may be, or where it may be applied, was considered 'elegant.' Complexity of detail, whether in a good or bad style of ornament, was approved as ' rich,' and with these two conditions of so-styled elegance and richness, the uneducated eye was satisfied. Recent advance in taste has shown that simplicity of form is not only the best for practical

reasons, but far more capable of artistic treatment than extravagant and cumbrous shapes.

The absurd fashion which regulates the arrangement of modern window-hangings cannot be too severely condemned, on account both of its ugliness and inconvenience. Curtains were originally hung across a window or door, not for the sake of ornament alone, but to exclude cold and draughts. They were suspended by little rings, which slipped easily over a stout metal rod—perhaps an inch or an inch and a half in diameter. Of course, between such a rod (stretched across the top of the window) and the ceiling, a small space must always intervene; and, therefore, to prevent the chance of wind blowing through in this direction, a boxing of wood became necessary, in front of which a plain valance was hung, sometimes cut into a vandyke-shaped pattern at its lower edge, but generally unplaited. As for the curtains themselves, when not in use they hung straight down on either side, of a sufficient length to touch, but not to sweep the ground.

Now, observe how we have burlesqued this simple and picturesque contrivance in our modern houses. The useful and convenient little rod has grown into a huge lumbering pole as thick as a man's arm, but not a whit stronger than its predecessor; for the pole is not only hollow, but constructed of metal far too thin in proportion to its diameter. Then, in place of the little finials which used to be fixed at each end of the rod to prevent the rings from slipping off, our modern upholsterer has substituted gigantic fuchsias, or other flowers, made of brass, gilt bronze, and even china, sprawling

downwards in a design of execrable taste.   Sometimes
this pole, being too weak for actual use, is fixed up simply
for ornament—or rather for pretentious show—while
the curtain really slides on an iron rod *behind* it.   Instead of the wooden boxing and valance, a gilt cornice,
or canopy, is introduced, contemptible in design, and
worse than useless in such a place ; for not only does it
afford, from the nature of its construction, no protection
against the draught behind, but, being made of thin,
sharp-edged metal, it is liable to cut and fray the curtain
which it crowns.   The curtains themselves are made
immoderately long, in order that they may be looped
up in clumsy folds over two large and eccentric-looking
metal hooks on either side of the window.   The result
of this needless and ugly complication is that in a
London house the curtains are seldom drawn : dust
gathers thickly in their folds, the stuff is prematurely
worn out, and comfort as well as artistic effect is sac-
rificed to meet a conventional notion of ' elegance.'

While on the subject of curtains, it may be as well
to add a few words regarding the employment of
fringe.   Fringe, as Pugin justly pointed out, was
originally nothing more than the threads of silk or
woollen stuff, knotted together at a ragged edge, to
prevent it from unravelling further.   By degrees they

came to be knotted at regular intervals, so that at length this contrivance grew into a system of ornament, which survived the necessity of its original adoption. But long after the use of detached fringe, it continued to be made of threads alone, and threads of the same quality as the stuff. Now, manufacturers have not only lost sight of the original *motive* of fringe, but they make it of fantastically turned pieces of wood, twisted round indiscriminately with silk and woollen thread ; and these are often attached to a valance scarcely deeper than the fringe itself! One may even see cord fringe sewn on stools, fire-screens, &c., where it is utterly inappropriate, and where, in short, no one but a modern upholsterer would ever think of putting it.

The lace trimmings and edgings used for 'antimacassars' and simple articles of household use are often open to objection on account of the flimsiness and extravagance of their design. It is a great pity that ladies who devote much of their time to the execution of the wretched patterns sold at 'fancy-work shops' do not exercise a little more discrimination in their choice. A little pains, together with a careful examination of old specimens to be found at the South Kensington Museum and elsewhere, would soon enable them to reform their taste in this respect, and to in-

form themselves of the general principles on which
such work should be designed and carried out. The
annexed specimen of hand-made lace is from the work
of a young lady who has given some attention to the
subject, and evidently with much profit. It will be

seen that the lace trimming is here divided into compartments which, though similar in general design,
display some variety of detail.   This is exactly in
accordance with the spirit of old and sound principles
of manufacture.

In the early part of this century, window-curtains
were only made of silk or damask.   The material

known as ' rep ' was next introduced, and was in many respects superior to what had been used before. But the Germans have invented a still better stuff—a mixture of silk, wool, and cotton—called *cotelan* in the shops, which is often worked in diaper patterns of excellent design. It is one of the most artistic examples of modern textile fabric now manufactured. To the French we are indebted for a heavy ribbed material decorated with broad bands or stripes of colour running transversely to its length, and resembling the pattern of a Roman scarf. This stuff has been much in vogue of late years, particularly among artists and people of good independent taste.

Another French material, called 'Algerine,' appeared for a short while in the London shops. It was made chiefly of cotton, and was also designed with horizontal stripes of colour on an unbleached white ground. In effect, it was all that could be wished, and it had, moreover, the additional advantage of being washable. But, of course, because it was cheap, and about the best thing of the kind which had appeared for many years, it found few admirers and but little demand. Having inquired for it at a well-known establishment, I was told that its manufacture had been discontinued, or, at all events, that no more could be procured from

France.* The new *cretonne* now used for bed furniture, &c., is a good substitute for chintz, in so far as it will wash, and does not depend for effect on a high glaze. Some excellent examples of this material, and printed calicos of artistic design, have been produced by W. Morris & Co., to whom the public are much indebted for improved taste in this branch of manufacture.

There is also a kind of damask made in plain colour—either green or crimson—enriched with stripes

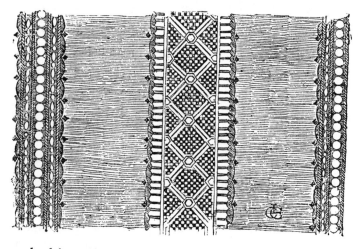

worked in various patterns with gold-coloured silk. It is not so expensive as *cotelan*, being much lighter in

* Since this was written, some varieties of the material have reappeared in the West-end shops.

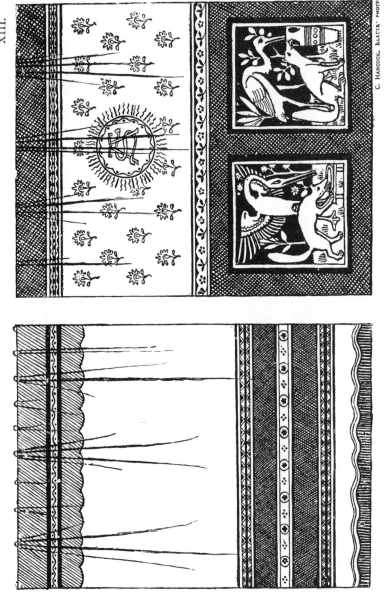

XIII.

Embroidered Portière Curtains,
designed by C. Heaton.

substance, but the design is very good. In this case the
stripes run parallel to the length of the curtain, and
thus give greater apparent height to the room in which
they are hung. Horizontal stripes, on the contrary,
have a tendency to make a low room look lower, though
it must be confessed that the folds of a curtain are
more agreeably defined in this manner than when the
stripes run parallel to them, and thus confuse the eye.

Some very beautiful specimens of *portière* curtains
were made some time ago from the respective designs of Mr. A. W. Blomfield and of Mr. C. Heaton.
They were composed of velvet and other stuffs,
embroidered by hand and decorated with deep
borders, consisting of alternate strips of velvet and
common horse-girths. It is a remarkable fact that
horse-girths (as well as certain kinds of coach-trim·
mings) traditionally preserve the spirit of some very
excellent designs, which have probably varied very
little, in pattern and general distribution of colour,
during the past century.

Two specimens of the curtains designed by Mr.
Heaton are here given in illustration. One of them is
decorated in *appliqué* work with a representation of
Æsop's fable, 'the Fox and the Stork.'

For summer curtains there is scarcely a better

material than that which is known in this country as
'Swiss lace.' It is made of stout thread-cotton, and
worked in two or three small but well-defined patterns.
It is apt to shrink a little in washing, but is otherwise
faultless in a practical point of view ; while in design
it is infinitely superior to the ordinary muslin curtain,
on which semi-naturalistic foliage and nondescript

ornament is allowed to meander after an extravagant
and meaningless fashion. It is not that 'nondescript'
ornament must necessarily be bad—it is not that semi-
naturalistic leaf-patterns are radically wrong in principle—but simply that English and French designers
were until recently unable to treat these elements of
decoration in a proper and artistic spirit.

Happily a great improvement has taken place within

the last few years in the character of almost every kind of textile fabric used for curtains and upholstery. Patterns, often of great artistic excellence and based upon a legitimate adaptation of form in vegetable life, are to be seen in the shop windows ; and skilful combinations of colour in secondary and tertiary tints, which it would have been impossible to procure a few years ago, may be found in *portières* and window-hangings in many varieties of material, and produced at a price which is quite within reach of ordinary means.* Speaking generally, one may say that this department of industrial art presents a far more hopeful prospect than any other for the advance of ' household taste.'

* I have supplied several designs for curtain stuffs to Messrs. Cowlishaw, Nicol & Co., of Manchester, as well as to Messrs. Jackson & Graham, of London.   Some of them are executed in material of very moderate cost.

Chapter IV.

THE FLOOR AND THE WALL.

ODERN manufacture may perhaps be said to
have received the greatest aid from science
at a period precisely when the arts of design
had sunk into their lowest degradation. A twofold
error sprang from this *mésalliance*. In the first place,
bad ornament was multiplied into vicious elaboration ;
and secondly, the eye became accustomed to appreciate and afterwards to desire a certain quality of
finish and ignoble neatness, which, while it is an almost
inevitable result of machinery in its perfected use, must
at the same time be utterly opposed to a free and
vigorous style of decoration. Every lady recognises
the superiority of hand-made lace and other textile
fabrics over those which are produced by artificial
means. The same criterion of excellence may be
applied to almost every branch of art-manufacture.
The perfect finish and accurate uniformity of shape —
the correct and even balance of pattern-form which

distinguish European goods from those of Eastern nations, and English goods especially from those of other countries in Europe—indicate degrees not only of advanced civilization, but, inversely, of decline in taste.

Our table-glass and porcelain, for example, have long been remarkable for pureness of material and symmetry of outline. Old Venetian glass and Italian majolica-ware were, on the contrary, seldom quite symmetrical in shape, or entirely free from natural defects. They depended for their beauty on qualities which cannot be tested by rule and compass, or be ensured by ordinary care. But the variety of their forms was endless, and every form had a grace and beauty of its own. The lovely colours with which they were invested may indeed, in some instances, have been the result of certain chemical combinations which modern science has failed to reproduce. But they owe their chief charm to the taste with which those colours were opposed to each other -- not to the evenness and equality of their tone. In fact, the very irregularity of form and inequality of tint which distinguish these objects of ancient art, conduced towards their real beauty; for they were the evidence of human handiwork, and that to the end of time will always be more interesting than the result of mechanical precision. Of course, division of labour and perfection of machinery have had their attendant advantages, and it cannot be denied that many articles of ancient luxury are by such aid now placed within reach of the million. But, although it would be undesirable, and indeed impossible, to reject in manufacture the appliances of modern science, we should be cautious of attaching too much importance in decorative art to those qualities of mere elaboration and finish which are independent of thought and manual labour.

The textile fabrics of Persia, Turkey, and India have long been famous for the graceful harmony with which their colours are blended. But, beyond a general uniformity of purpose which is preserved in the design, the whole system of their ornament is absolutely careless. Examine any old and good specimen of an Eastern carpet, and you will probably find a border on the right in which the stripes are twice as broad as those on the left. There are exactly thirteen of these queer-looking angular flowers at this end of the room ; over the way there are only twelve. At the north corner, near the window, that zigzag line ends in a little circle ; at the south, in a square ; at the east, in a dot; at the west, there is nothing at all. This is in the true spirit of good and noble design. On the Continent, as well as in this country, Oriental goods are often imitated; but the imitation is a failure, because the English and French designers look with

disdain on the irregularity of Eastern work. In their eyes nothing can be quite beautiful of which the two opposite sides are not precisely alike. Accordingly the whole carpet is planned, line for line and spot for spot, with studied accuracy throughout. The result, no doubt, will be found mathematically correct by anyone who takes the trouble to measure it, but the vigour and independence of the original are utterly lost in the copy.

Choose, then, the humblest type of Turkey carpet or the cheapest hearthrug from Scinde, and be sure they will afford you more lasting eye-pleasure than any English imitation. As for the specimens of our own peculiar national taste in textile art—the rose-wreaths —the malachite marble patterns—the crimson *moire antique* with borders of shaded vine-leaves—the thousand-and-one pictorial monstrosities which you see displayed in the windows of Oxford Street and Ludgate Hill—they are only fit to cover the floor of Madame Tussaud's Chamber of Horrors.

It is curious that the English, who take pains that the patterns of their carpets shall be worked out with such nice accuracy, should be quite indifferent to the symmetry of their general outline. Except in the dining-room of an English house, one rarely sees such a thing as a square—or rather a *rectangular—* carpet. Two sides of it at least are sure to be notched and chopped about in order that they may fit into the various recesses caused by windows and the projection of the chimney-breast. This is essentially a modern fashion, and a very objectionable one.

In the first place, much of the material is cut (as the phrase goes) 'to waste.' Secondly, a carpet once laid down in a room will never suit another (although it is often convenient to make such changes) without further alterations. Thirdly, the practice of entirely covering up the floor, and thus leaving no evidence of its material, is contrary to the first principles of decorative art, which require that the nature of construction, so far as is possible, should always be revealed, or at least indicated, by the ornament which it bears. No one wants a carpet in the nooks and corners of a room; and it is pleasant to feel that there, at all events, the floor can assert its independence. It is true that the colour of deal boards, especially when they become old and dirty, is by no means satisfactory, but a little of the staining-fluid now in common use will meet this difficulty at a merely nominal cost.

The floors of good old French mansions were often inlaid with variously-coloured wood arranged in geometrical patterns. This branch of decorative art, known as *parquetry*, has been of late years revived in England, and is much in vogue at country houses. Parquetry floor-borders are now supplied at a price which is scarcely greater per superficial foot than that paid for a good Brussels carpet. With such a border projecting two or three feet from the wall all round, the carpet need not be carried into the recesses and corners of a room, but may be left square at the sides. It is hardly necessary to say that the effect of this arrangement, including as it does the additional grace of inlaid woodwork, is infinitely more artistic and in-teresting than that which the ordinary system presents.

The annexed illustrations are from specimens of parquetry floors and floor-borders, manufactured by Mr. Arrowsmith of Bond Street, whose name has been creditably associated with the revival of this art.

With regard to the style of the carpet, it may be assumed that, except in a few rare instances, where an European influence has been brought to bear on the manufacture of the East, all Oriental work is excellent. Care should be taken, however, to avoid those designs which are remarkable for over-brilliance of colour. They are apt to be inharmonious with the rest of the furniture, and rich Oriental dyes frequently have a deleterious effect on the material which they stain. The crimson used in Scinde rugs, for instance, is especially destructive, and the portions dyed with this colour wear out long before the rest. The dull Indian red is far more enduring, and is also more likely to blend well with the surrounding tints.

W. PICKES, SC.

Parquetry Floor Borders,
Manufactured by A. J, Arrowsmith.

Parquetry Floor Borders,
Manufactured by A. J. Arrowsmith.

Turkey carpets are hardly dearer than the best productions of this country, but there are some English carpets—those known as Kidderminster for instance— of excellent patterns and, of course, much cheaper than any which can be imported from abroad. There is no

reason why true principles of design should not be found in the humblest object of household use, and, so far as European goods are concerned, it not unfrequently happens that the commonest material is invested with the best form and colour. Carpets are no exception to this rule. In London shops their artistic

worth is at present a matter of mere chance, and is
certainly independent of all pecuniary considerations.
The simplest diapered grounds are the best, and it is
desirable that the prevailing tint of a carpet should

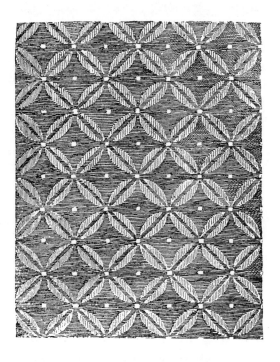

contrast rather than repeat that of the wall-paper.
Large sprawling patterns, however attractive they may
be in colour, should be avoided as utterly destructive
of effect to the furniture which is placed on them, and,

above all, every description of shaded ornament should
be sternly banished from our floors.

Next to the mistakes committed in the design of
carpets, there are few artistic solecisms more apparent

than those which the paper-stainers perpetrate by way
of decoration. Concerning taste, as the old Latin adage
informs us, there is no disputing ; and if people *will*
prefer a bouquet of flowers or a group of spaniels

worked upon their hearthrug to the conventional patterns which are adopted by the Indian and Turkish weavers, it is difficult to convince them of their error. We require no small amount of art instruction and experience to see *why* the direct imitation of natural objects is wrong in ornamental design. The *quasi-*fidelity with which the forms of a rose or a bunch of ribbons, or a ruined castle, can be reproduced on carpets, crockery, and wall-papers will always possess a certain kind of charm for the uneducated eye, just as the mimicry of natural sounds in music, from the rolling of thunder to the cackling of poultry, will delight a vulgar ear. Both are ingenious, amusing, attractive for the moment, but neither lie within the legitimate province of art.

Now, about the time that the famous 'Battle of Prague' became a favourite exercise with youthful pianists, and fathers and brothers were daily bored with the musical imitations of roar of cannon, clashing of swords, trample of horses, and shrieks of the dying —at a period, I say, when all these deplorable con-sequences of war were brought before us in a most emphatic and præ-Raphaelite manner on Mr. Broad-wood's well-known instruments by young ladies of an age varying from ten to sixteen—just at this epoch the worst style of art which this country has ever seen prevailed throughout the whole field of design. Upholstery was in bad taste; glass and china were in bad taste; cabinet-work was in bad taste. But of all the ugly fashions of that day, by far the most contemptible was that of paperhangings. Now and then, in tearing down the paper from old walls where it has been allowed to accumulate (a very slovenly and unhealthy practice, by the way), the workmen, after removing two or three layers of paste, &c., will come upon a curious specimen of mural decoration, which embodies in its pattern sometimes a suggestion of landscape; sometimes a bit of ornamental gardening in impossible perspective; sometimes a group of foreign birds, repeated at regular intervals; but often a curious combination of those diverse elements of design, mixed up with huge flowers and creeping plants, meandering over the whole surface of the wall.

Such were the eccentricities which the last generation affected, and which are, I need scarcely add, all widely removed from true principles of taste. Indeed, common sense points to the fact, that as a wall represents the flat surface of a solid material which forms part of the construction of a house, it should be decorated after a manner which will belie neither its flatness nor solidity.   For this reason all shaded ornament and patterns, which by their arrangement of colour give an appearance of relief, should be strictly avoided.   Where natural forms are introduced, they should be treated in a conventional manner—i.e. drawn in outline, and filled in with flat colour, which may be 'hatched' over with lines here and there to express form, but without attempt at pictorial gradation.   No doubt many excellent examples of arabesque and other surface-decoration, as at Pompeii and in the Loggie of the Vatican, may be cited, where a certain degree of roundness has been aimed at in the case of animal form ; but such examples excel not *because* of their style, but in spite of it.   Moreover, it must be remembered that these paintings were the actual handiwork of consummate artists; and as we cannot hope to imitate, by machine-printed paper, the refinement of manual skill, it is better that we should limit our designs to those forms which need no such delicacy of treatment.

In the Middle Ages it was customary to decorate the walls of the most important rooms of a public building or private mansion with tapestry ; and there is no doubt that a rich and picturesque effect was thus obtained which no other means could produce.   But it is obvious that the mere expense of such a practice, to say nothing of the consideration of cleanliness (especially in town-houses, where dust collects with great rapidity), would render it out of the question for modern appliance. In later times stencil-painting was the first step towards a simpler style of mural ornament, and indeed it is still in vogue throughout Italy and other parts of the Continent. It consists, as some of my readers may be aware, of applying flatted colour to a wall with a brush over perforated plates of zinc or other metal. These perforations may be cut into an endless variety of patterns ; and certainly a plaster surface thus decorated has many advantages over one which has been lined with paper, particularly in a warm climate. The plates too, when once prepared for a satisfactory design, may be used again at pleasure elsewhere, and the space between the diapered patterns thus formed may be varied to suit the size of the room. Still, it must be confessed that the more recent invention of paperhangings supplies a cheaper, readier, and, to our English notions of comfort, a more satisfactory means of internal decoration.

There has been a very great improvement of late in this branch of manufacture. Pugin led the way by designing some excellent examples for the Houses of

Parliament and elsewhere; and since his time many architects have thought it worth while to design appropriate wall-papers for the houses which they have built. By degrees manufacturers took the matter up, and adopted the patterns suggested by qualified artists, and the result is that good and well-designed papers may now be had at a very reasonable price. Of course, many wretched specimens continue to be displayed, for the selection of customers whose taste is of too lofty and independent a character to be influenced by any guiding principle; but, nevertheless, good papers are to be found by those who choose to look for them.* In this, as in every branch of art-manufacture, it is for the shops to lead the way towards reform. The British public are, as a body, utterly incapable of distinguishing good from bad design, and have not time to enquire into principles. As long as gaudy and extravagant trash is displayed in the windows of our West-end thoroughfares, so long will it attract ninety-nine people out of every hundred to buy. But let customers once become familiar with the sight of good forms and judicious combinations of

* Messrs. Jeffrey & Co., of Essex Road, Islington, and Mr. H. Woollams, of High Street, Marylebone, have produced some excellent paper-hangings in great variety of design.

colour, and we may one day aspire to the formation of a national taste.

But to return to my subject: the choice of a wall-paper should be guided in every respect by the destination of the room in which it will be used. The most important question will always be whether it is to form a decoration in itself, or whether it is to become a mere background for pictures. In the latter case the paper can hardly be too subdued in tone. Very light stone colour or green (not emerald), and silver-grey will be found suitable for this purpose, and two shades of the *same colour* are generally sufficient for one paper. In drawing-rooms, embossed white or cream colour, with a very small diapered pattern, will not be amiss, where water-colour drawings are hung. As a rule, the simplest patterns are the best for every situation; but where the eye has to rest upon the surface of the wall alone, a greater play of line in the ornament may become advisable. It is obvious that delicate tints admit of more linear complexity than those which are rich or dark. Intricate forms should be accompanied by quiet colour, and variety of hue should be chastened by the plainest possible outlines. In colour, wall-papers should relieve without violently opposing that of the furniture and hangings by which they are surrounded.

There should be one dominant hue in the room, to which all others introduced are subordinate. This will admit of many variations of shade, passing from green to blue, or venetian red to brown, without requiring absolute uniformity of tint throughout. Some people conceive that the most important condition of good taste has been fulfilled if every bit of damask in one room is cut from the same piece, and every article of furniture is made of the same wood. At this rate the art of outfitting would be reduced to a very simple process. The real secret of success in decorative colour is, however, quite as much dependent on subtle variations and delicate contrast as on similarity of tint; nor can real artistic effect be expected without the employment of both.

Nothing is more difficult than to estimate the value and intensity of colour when spread over a large surface from the simple inspection of a pattern-book. The purchaser will frequently find that a paper which he has ordered will look either darker or lighter when hung than it appeared in the piece. For this reason it is advisable to suspend several lengths of the paper side by side *in the room* for which it is intended, and it is only by this means that a notion of the ultimate effect can be arrived at. In the early part of this cen-

tury it was a common practice to carry
round the principal rooms of a house to
about three feet from the floor, where it w;
by a little wooden moulding. The paper was then
only required to cover the upper part of the walls, and
the effect was far less monotonous than now, when it
is carried down to our feet. The old fashion had an
additional advantage in protecting the wall from
contact with chairs and careless fingers, which generally disfigure delicately-tinted paperhangings. This
picturesque old feature of high wainscoting has long
been banished, with many others, from modern households, but, to protect walls from being rubbed by furniture, narrow strips of wood may be nailed down to
the floor within an inch or two of the wall. The legs
of chairs (and consequently their back-rails) are thus
kept off from the paper behind them, and a ' grazing-
line ' is avoided.

As 'diaper' designs have been more than once
referred to in these pages, it may be as well to explain
that they belong to that class of patterns which are
either definitely enclosed by bounding lines, or at least
divided into compartments of a uniform size throughout. These compartments or ' diapers ' are often of a
geometrical form, and in that case may either be round or

square, diamond-shaped or *quatrefoiled* in outline. The best are those in which segmental curves are blended with angular forms. For ordinary sized rooms they should not exceed five or six inches across in any direction, but for bedrooms, &c., much less will suffice. It should be borne in mind that nothing dwarfs the size of rooms so much as large-patterned papers. Without attempting to arrive at any definite rule for the choice of patterns, we may safely avoid some altogether, and among them is that species of decoration which may be included under the head of 'scroll' ornament. It will be easily recognised from its resemblance to the so-called carved work round modern drawing-room mirrors, to which I have already alluded, and is sure to be of bad style.

The leaves of certain plants, when appropriately treated, become excellent decorative forms. Of these, ivy, maple, crowfoot, oak, and fig-leaves are well adapted for the purpose. Where two shades of the same colour are employed, and quietness of effect is especially desired, the overlaid tint should be but very little darker than the ground; and if drawings, &c., are to be hung upon it, the pattern should be hardly discernible from a little distance.

Pugin, in his designs for mediæval paperhangings,

Wall Paper manufactured by Jeffrey & Co.
from a design by Charles L. Eastlake

Wall Paper manufactured by Jeffrey & Co.
from a design by Charles L. Eastlake

Wall Paper manufactured by Jeffrey & Co.
from a design by B. Binyon

XIX.

Scale : about one-eighth real size.

Part of a Mural Decoration for Frieze, executed by Heaton, Butler, & Co.
Designed by C. Heaton. Subject—' The Fox without a Tail.'

no doubt borrowed largely from the ancient diaper patterns employed during the Middle Ages for surface-decoration, and of which, perhaps, the Early Italian school of painting affords the best examples. Of late years, however, there has been a growing distaste for mediæval patterns, and—as in curtain stuffs—the present tendency of design is in the direction of natural forms chiefly adapted from flowering plants. The accompanying plates illustrate designs for wall-papers manufactured by Messrs. Jeffreys & Co., one partaking of the diapered character, and the other two based on studies of ivy and the 'solanum' shrub.

Paperhangings should in no case be allowed to cover the whole space of a wall from skirting to ceiling. A 'dado,' or plinth space of plain colour, either in paper or distemper, should rise to a height of three or four feet from the floor. This may be separated from the diapered paper above by a light wood moulding stained or ebonized. A second space, of frieze, left just below the ceiling, and filled with arabesque ornament painted on a distemper-ground, is always effective, but of course involves some additional expense. The most dreary method of decorating the wall of a sitting-room is to cover it all over with an unrelieved pattern of monotonous design.

Gold, when judiciously introduced, may be a valuable adjunct in the design of paperhangings. It frequently, however, doubles, and sometimes trebles, the price of a piece. Of the cheaper sort very good designs may now be had at from threepence to sixpence per yard. But for a shilling or eighteenpence a yard, papers may now be procured which are not only luxurious in effect, but of high artistic excellence.

Messrs. Morris, Marshall and Co., of Queen Square Bloomsbury, have produced some admirable examples of this latter class, specimens of which, as well as of the chaste and beautiful stained glass manufactured by the same firm, have been used in the decoration of the new refreshment-rooms at South Kensington Museum.

Some of the French papers, embossed after the manner of old stamped leather, are very effective if cut up into oblong pieces about two feet in length and enclosed in wood panels just underneath the cornice, so as to form a kind of frieze decoration round the room. It is true that if this embossed paper be regarded as a mere imitation of leather, its use is hardly consistent with principles illumined by what Mr. Ruskin has called the Lamp of Truth. But, after all, the manufacture of paperhangings is essentially a modern art, and even in its origin typified tapestry or stencil painting. It would be hypercritical therefore to prescribe any limits to its adaptation for decorative purposes beyond those which are necessarily imposed by the nature of the material and the process of manufacture. To go further than this in any branch of art would lead to a sort of æsthetic Pharisaism.

Chapter V.

THE LIBRARY.

F all the rooms in a modern house, that which is used as a library or study is the one least like to offend a fastidious taste by its appointments.   Here at least the furniture—usually of oak—is strong and solid.   The silly knick-knacks which too frequently crowd a drawing-room table, cheffonier, or mantelpiece are banished from this retreat.   The ormolu and compo-gilt decoration which prevails upstairs is voted, even by upholsterers, out of place on the ground-floor; and those stern arbiters of taste even go so far as to recommend a Turkey carpet or a sober-pattern 'Brussels' instead of the tangled maze of flowers and ribbons which we have to tread on elsewhere.   Yet, with all these advantages, our library, especially in a modern-sized London house, is often dull and uninteresting.   The bookshelves, cupboards, writing-table, and other articles of furniture which it contains are of a uniform and stereotyped appearance, and never rise beyond the level of intense respectability. This is due to various causes, but among others to the foolish practice of varnishing new oak before it has acquired the rich and varied tint which time and use alone can give it. Wood treated in this way keeps clean, it is true, but never exhibits that full beauty of grain which adds so much to its picturesqueness. The best plan is to rub the natural surface of the wood well over with a little oil from time to time and so leave it. This will reveal its vein without varnish, and allow it in due course to become deeper in colour. The construction of the bookshelves themselves would appear to be simple and straightforward, and yet it is astonishing how many practical mistakes are blindly perpetuated by cabinet-makers of the present day, who have widely departed from the principles of old joinery. It might be tedious, in these pages, to point out such mistakes as are of a purely technical nature. But there are some so opposed to common sense that they call for special mention.

For instance, mouldings were originally employed to decorate surfaces of wood or stone, which sloped either vertically or horizontally from one plane to another. Thus, the mouldings of a door represent the bevelled or chamfered edge of the stout framework

which holds the slighter panels. It is obvious, therefore, that these mouldings ought to be worked in the
solid wood, and form part of the framework referred to.
Instead of this, in modern cabinet work they are
detached slips of wood, glued into their places after the
door has been actually put together. To such an
absurdity is the system carried, that these *applied*
mouldings are often allowed to project beyond the
surface of the door-frame, and not unfrequently are
repeated in the centre of the panel itself. The same
fault may be found with the cornice which crowns the
bookcase. It pretends to be solid framing, whereas in
nine cases out of ten it could be pulled to pieces by
a child's hand. The hinges, too, of cabinet doors are
lamentably weak, and the reason of this is, that such
hinges are reduced to a *minimum* in size, and kept out
of sight. The old hinges were not cramped for space,
but boldly stretched across the door-frame, which they
thus well supported. Moreover, their form was usually
ornamental, and in brass or iron they contrasted well
with the colour of the wood to which they were fixed.
Luckily, there are metal-workers now of whom such
hinges may be bought, together with lock escutcheons,
keys, 'closing rings,' and all the proper fittings for a
cabinet door. They are, however, expensive, and far

more expensive than they need be if such objects were more in demand.

It is usual for the lower shelves alone to be enclosed by doors, the upper ones being left open for easy access to books. There are several ways of fixing these shelves. They may either rest upon ledges, which are supported in their turn by upright slips of wood notched at regular intervals, or they may slide into grooves sunk in the frames which hold them, or they may be sustained by little brass brackets or 'shelf-rings,' so arranged as to leave no projection which can interfere with books at the corner. The last is a modern invention, more remarkable for its ingenuity than for much practical advantage. When grooves are sunk, care should be taken to increase the thickness of the side-pieces, which otherwise become dangerously weak. The shelves themselves should never be less than an inch in thickness for a span of four feet. A little leather valance should always be nailed against their outer edges. This not only protects the books from dust, but when the leather is scalloped and stamped in gilt patterns, it adds considerably to the general effect.

For material, oak is by far the best wood to use both for appearance and durability. Unpolished mahogany acquires a good colour with age. It also looks very well stained black and covered with a thin varnish. The hinges, escutcheons, &c., should then be of white metal. Stained deal, as a cheap substitute for oak, may answer in places where it is not liable to be rubbed or handled; but for library wear it cannot be recommended, since it shows every scratch on its surface, and soon becomes shabby with use. When, for economy's sake, deal is employed, it is better to paint it in flatted colour, because this can be renewed from time to time, whereas wood once stained and varnished must remain as it is. Indian red and bluish green are perhaps the best general tints for wood when used for ordinary domestic fittings, but these may be effectively relieved by patterns and borders of white or yellow. Sometimes a mere line introduced here and there to define the construction, with an angle ornament (which may be *stencilled*) at the corners, will be sufficient. In all chromatic decoration, I need scarcely say that bright and violent hues *en masse* should be avoided.

With regard to the association of tints, it would not be difficult to quote from Chevreul, and others who have given scientific reasons for their various theories —who teach that blue is best suited for concave surfaces, and yellow for those which are convex—that the primary colours should be used on the upper portions of objects, and the secondary and tertiary on the lower.* But, unfortunately, most of these precepts, however ingeniously they may be based on science, are continually belied by Nature, which is, after all, the best and truest authority on this subject. It has indeed been argued that all who consult her works with love and attention, will in time appreciate the right value of decorative colour, and that those who have learnt in that school need learn in no other. But this seems to be a conclusion which is not founded on practical experience. The conditions of beauty in pictorial art are widely remote from those which are fulfilled in judicious decoration. An accurate knowledge of the proportions of the human form is doubtless indispensable to the education of an architect; but it will not of itself enable him to determine the best proportions for a building. No one is better acquainted with the subtle charms of Nature's colour than a good landscape painter; but what landscape painter—as such—could

* The question whether, after all, yellow is, and whether green is not, a primary hue, has been recently raised by the ingenious theories of Mr. Wm. Benson ; and the new light which he has thrown on the subject of colour generally may, in some degrees, explain the difficulties hitherto felt in reconciling scientific data with principles of taste in chromatic decoration.

be trusted to design a paper for his drawing-room wall?
The blue sky which is over our heads and the green
grass which springs beneath our feet would not, even
if we could match the delicacy of their hues, afford us a
strict and perfect precedent for the colour of our floors
and ceilings; nor are the fairest flowers which bloom
suitable objects to be copied literally for surface ornament. The art of the decorator is to *typify*, not to
represent, the works of Nature, and it is just the difference between this artistic abstraction and pseudo-
realism which separates good and noble design from
that which is commonplace and bad.

There is usually a kind of frieze running round the
top of a bookcase, between the books and the cornice
above them. This space may well be decorated with
painted ornament in the form of arabesques, armorial
bearings, and appropriate texts. Any of these would
be far more pleasant to look at than the cold and
formally-moulded panels into which this part is usually
divided. The pilasters also (I use the generally accepted term), which separate one compartment of the
bookcase from another, might be effectively treated in
the same manner.

It used to be the fashion to place a plaster urn or
bust at the top of each bookcase, to give what up-

holsterers call a 'finish' to the room. Urns are, however, but meaningless things in these days of Christian burial; and busts at so high an elevation, especially in a small room, convey a very distorted notion of the features which they represent. Large china bowls and vases may, however, be seen to advantage in such a place, and failing them, statuettes may be recommended. Good plaster casts, about two feet high, copied from the antique, may now be procured for five or six shillings a-piece, and such figures as the Gladiator, the Discobolos, and the Antinous, would probably form a much better 'finish' for the top of a bookcase than the gloomy urn which was once in vogue.

Unless the cases are intended for books of great value or for those rarely referred to, it is hardly advisable to enclose them with glass doors; such an expedient often involves unnecessary trouble, and may prevent ready access to books when every moment is of value to the reader. Two doors may be opened at the same time and come in contact so as to break the glass, &c. After all, books are required for use, not for ornament, and if handled carefully, will last for more than one generation, even without the protection of a glass case.

A library table, open under the centre, and fitted on either side with a set of useful little drawers, is, of course, indispensable to the room. This piece of furniture, so commonly met with in upholsterers' shops, is a singularly unobjectionable specimen of English manufacture. It has some of the inevitable faults of modern joinery, viz., adhesive mouldings, ' mitred ' joints, &c. ; but taken as a whole it is not unpicturesque. Its upper surface is usually covered with leather, glued to the table-top all over, within an inch or so of its edge. The colour of this leather should either match or contrast well with that of the curtains and carpets in the room. Green is incomparably the best suited to oak.

There is no better kind of seat for a library than the ' Cromwell ' chair, which has already been described, and the general form of which dates, no doubt, from the seventeenth century, although it has since undergone various modifications in regard to detail. Old examples of this chair are still to be met with in farmhouses and country cottages, and their framework, at least, can be copied at a trifling cost by any intelligent country carpenter.

At the beginning of this chapter it was observed that ' knick-knacks ' were usually banished from the

Library Bookcase,
executed by Jackson & Graham from a design by Charles L. Eastlake.

Mantelpiece Shelves,
executed by Jackson & Graham from a design by Charles L. Eastlake.

library. By that expression I meant to include that
heterogeneous assemblage of modern rubbish which,
under the head of ' Dresden china' and various other
names, finds its way into the drawing-room or boudoir.
But my readers must not therefore suppose that I
intended to discourage the collection of really good
specimens of art manufacture. The smallest example
of rare old porcelain, of ivory carving, of ancient metal-
work, of enamels, of Venetian glass, of anything which
illustrates good design and skilful workmanship, should
be acquired whenever possible, and treasured with the
greatest care. It is impossible to overrate the influence
which such objects may have in educating the eye to
appreciate what really constitutes good art. An Indian
ginger-jar, a Flemish beer-jug, a Japanese fan, may
each become in turn a valuable lesson in decorative
form and colour.

By and by there will be more to say on this subject.
Meanwhile I would suggest to those who possess such
things that they should associate and group them
together as much as possible. A set of narrow shelves
ranged at the back, and forming part of the dining-
room sideboard, would be admirable for this purpose,
and would certainly form a very picturesque feature
in the room. Failing this arrangement (and one may

imagine certain conventional prejudices being brought
to bear against it), perhaps the library would be the next
best repository for such objects.   Few men care for a
mirror in such a room ; but, if it is indispensable to the
mantel-piece, let it be a long low strip of glass, stretching across the width of the chimney-breast, about
eighteen inches in height, and divided into panels.
Over this may be raised a capital set of narrow shelves
—say six inches wide and twelve inches apart—for
specimens of old china, &c.   The plates should be
placed upright on their edges, and may be easily prevented from slipping off by a shallow groove sunk in
the thickness of each shelf.   A little museum may
thus be formed, and remain a source of lasting pleasure
to its possessors, seeing that 'a thing of beauty is a
joy for ever.'

The most formidable obstacle which lies in the way
of any attempt to reform the arts of design in this
country, is perhaps the indifference with which people
of even reputed taste are accustomed to regard the
products of common industry.   There is many a
connoisseur of pictures and of sculpture, many a
virtuoso now haunting auctions and curiosity shops
with a view to gratify his particular hobby, who would
be surprised if he were asked to pass his opinion on

the merits of a door-knocker or set of fire-irons. By such people—and they represent a very numerous class—art can only be valued as an end in itself, and not as the means to an end. The sense of pleasure, which in civilised life we derive from fair forms and colour, is to a great extent instinctive ; but in so far as it is the result of education, it seems absurd to limit its range of enjoyment to this or that field of human labour. What should we think of a musical amateur who, while fully able to appreciate the performance of a Joachim, could listen with indifference to the machine-made melodies of a grinding organ, or hear with approval a pianoforte played out of time and tune ? Yet this is exactly what people do who praise the works of Leighton and Millais at the Royal Academy Exhibition, and go straightway off to the shops to buy and fill their houses with articles of manufacture which are distinguished not only by an absence of real beauty, but by the presence of much definite ugliness.

Even where a tolerable taste for upholstery exists, it does not descend to details. We have come to take the form and fashion of some minor objects of ordinary use upon trust, or rather we have ceased to associate them with the interests of art altogether.

This state of things, no doubt, is due to a popular conviction that in the case of certain practical appliances it would be impossible to unite convenience with anything like artistic design ; that any attempt to do so would be equally fatal to both, and that the carpenter and metal-worker must know, better than we can teach them, the conditions and requirements of their trades.* But all this is surely erroneous. So far from good design being under any circumstances incompatible with strong and sturdy service, it is only in bad design that use is not kept in view as the first and guiding principle in manufacture. The artizans' work of a former age is interesting chiefly because it is pre-eminently *practical* work. Our own mechanics' work becomes *mean* chiefly when its ultimate object is lost sight of in the endeavour to get things up cheaply, or give them an appearance which belies their purpose.

This is especially the case with modern ironmongery and common metal work. Let us take the familiar instance of an ordinary house door, and note how the hinges are kept carefully out of sight, as if they were something to be ashamed of. It is almost impossible

---

* I allude here, of course, to *modern* handicraft. There was a time when every workman was to some extent an artist, and might be safely trusted with the details of any design which he was called upon to execute.

to construct such hinges as these which shall be of
sufficient strength to support a door of any important
weight.   Hence the not unfrequent expense and discomfort occasioned by doors drooping at the end
furthest from the hinge.   The carpenter is called in,
perhaps to shift the lock ' catch,' or to shave the lower
edge of the door.   This, of course, must leave a corresponding gap above.   In course of time the hinge is
partially torn from its screw holes, and a further outlay
required.   Now the old hinges were not ' half butts,'
as our ordinary ones are called, but stout straps of iron,
which, more or less decorated, stretched across the surface of the door on either side, and being bolted
through the thickness, gave it ample support.   Very
beautiful examples of this hinge may still be seen on
old church doors, and even in modern farm-buildings the
type is still preserved, though in a ruder way.   The
ancient locks too, instead of being concealed and let
into the door by cutting away, and thus weakening the
lock rail as in the modern fashion, were boldly attached
to its outer surface, and were often, as well as the keys
which belonged to them, objects of real art in their
way.   The bolts and ' spindle ' handles of the ordinary
modern door are always getting out of order, besides
being generally ill-designed.   Bolts should not be let

into the thickness of a door, but appear in their proper
place on its surface.   Some of the ' art metal-workers '
are giving their attention to the manufacture of ' door
furniture,' which without being Gothic or ecclesiastical
in appearance, is treated after an artistic fashion.   The

annexed cuts represent brass 'finger plates,' manufactured by Messrs. Benham & Froud.   They are of
sheet metal, pierced and engraved in patterns.

There is, perhaps, no branch of English trade more
prolific in design than that of the furnishing iron-
monger.   The variety of patterns which Birmingham
and other manufacturing districts supply in the way of

stoves, fenders, fire-irons, gas pendants, moderator lamps, coal-scuttles, umbrella-stands, &c., &c., is truly astonishing. In a large establishment for the sale of such goods the eye is positively bewildered by a multitude of objects, most of them extravagant in style, and possessing that ephemeral kind of attractiveness which is the result of polish and lacquer. One may see people in such shops perplexed and wearied with inspecting one article after another, as the shopman drones out his oft-repeated remarks that this is 'elegant,' that 'very handsome,' the other 'just the thing for a drawing-room,' and so forth.

Although the style of drawing-room fenders, as I have mentioned, is improving, those intended for the library and dining-room are often coarse and clumsy in design. Manufacturers will persist in decorating them with a species of cast-iron ornament, which looks like a bad imitation of rococo carved work. Almost all cast-iron ornament (excepting the delicate patterns in very low relief, such as one sometimes sees on an old Sussex stove) is hopelessly ugly. The crisp leafy decoration, and vigorous scrolls of ancient iron-work, were produced by the hammer and pliers. Bolts, straps, nails, and rivets, the proper and legitimate means of connecting the several parts, were never concealed, but were introduced and enriched in such a manner as not only to serve a practical purpose, but to become decorative features in themselves.

By way of contrast to the unworkmanlike spirit of ordinary manufacture, I give two sketches of fenders for a dining-room and library designed by Mr. A. W. Blomfield. They are exceedingly simple in construction, and fully answer the purpose for which (as its

very name signifies) a *fender* is intended, namely, to
protect dresses, &c., from the chance of becoming
ignited by close contact with the fire—an accident,

unfortunately, of too frequent occurrence while the
dangerous and ungraceful crinoline was in fashion.

The next illustration is that of a charcoal brazier, in
the possession of Lord Mount Edgcumbe at Cothele.
It is of modern Spanish manufacture, and was purchased
at the International Exhibition of 1862. When we
compare such work as this with the tawdry decoration

and unpicturesque forms which objects of similar use in England are allowed to assume, it is impossible to help regretting that the old traditions of design in our own metal work, based as they were upon propriety and convenience of form, have been of late years so

much neglected. This Spanish brazier is worthy of the sixteenth century, and is probably identical in general form with the 'chafing-dishes' of that period. It is admirably adapted for its purpose, and the manufacturer has kept that steadily in view, as well as the nature of the material with which he has had to deal—an essential condition of all good design.

I remember seeing in the Cathedral of Orvieto an iron gate of exquisite workmanship, which, being very heavy, required the support of what is called a stay-bar, or rod running in a diagonal direction from the hinge-post to the top rail. A similar contrivance may be seen in our own wooden field-gates. Well, the old Italian smith, though quite an artist in his way, sensibly bore in mind the real *purpose* of his stay-bar, and instead of twisting a serpent or a mermaid about it, as a modern designer would have been likely to do, he kept his rod stout and round, except just at one point, where, in order to express precisely the sort of work it had to do, he fashioned the iron into the quaint likeness of a human hand nervously clutching at and *holding up* the gate below. Now, if we compare the apt ingenuity of this notion with the stupid wreaths and arrow-heads and lictors' *fasces* which one sees introduced in the design of our iron railings, we shall, I think, see one reason why the spirit of old handicraft was superior to the pedantry and weakness of modern workmanship.

Among familiar objects of household use, I do not know a more contemptible instance of perverted taste than the ordinary tea or coffee-urn of an English break-fast-table. It is generally a debased copy from some antique base, the original being executed in marble or earthenware, and therefore quite unfit for reproduction in metal. In order to add to its attractions, the lid and handles are probably decorated *à la Pompadour*, and, to complete the absurdity, a thoroughly modern tap is inserted in the bowl. What is, after all, the use of a breakfast urn? If it is to contain hot water, a good swing-kettle with a spirit-lamp underneath is far more useful; if it is intended to hold tea or coffee, surely a tea or coffee-pot is a better and simpler vessel for the purpose. The same sort of pseudo-classicism may be noticed in the design of ordinary gaseliers and moderator lamps. The urn type not unfrequently reappears in them, combined with ex-traordinary versions of the inevitable acanthus-leaf, as if in the whole range of vegetable life this was the only kind of foliage worth imitating. There is a lumpy *unmetallic* look about the ornament, which no amount of elaboration can relieve. The reason of this is that it has been either cast in separate pieces and then chased up, or (in the case of brass) stamped out of the thinnest possible metal (often not thicker than a piece of paper), and then brazed together in such a manner as to look like a solid mass. Now, there can be no objection to a moderate thinness of substance in the execution of metallic ornament. Indeed it is, as

I have said, one of the legitimate conditions to be observed in the artistic treatment of this material ; but

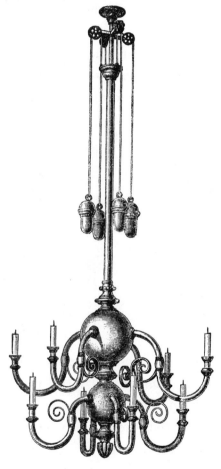

then one ought to be able to perceive at once that it *is*
thin, and the ornamental portions should be designed

consistently with that fact.   To invest metal-work
with forms which might be as well executed in wood
or stone, is to lose sight of the first principle of good
design.

Gas fittings are of comparatively recent origin, and
belong to those requirements of modern life with which
our forefathers managed to dispense.   There is, how-

ever, no reason why such subjects should be of the
commonplace and stereotyped forms usually adopted
in ordinary dwelling-houses.   Nor, on the other hand,
is it necessary that they should assume the ecclesiastical
shapes generally found in the art metal-worker's catalogue.   The annexed woodcuts illustrate a 'Sconce'
light and three different kinds of gas-bracket adapted

for domestic use, and manufactured by Messrs. Benham and Froud, who have lately turned their attention to this special department of their art. Specimens of work executed by the same firm are represented on the last pages of this chapter, viz. two chimneypiece spill-vases, of brass, decorated with engraved and pierced ornament. The bell-lever on page 155 is also made by the same firm.

Public taste is often very perverse and inconsistent as to the choice and appliance of material and ornament. For instance, there was, not many years ago, a great demand

for bronze candlesticks, whereas brass is a far more brilliant material for the purpose, and is capable of being treated with greater richness of form and surface-decoration. But on fire-stoves and grates, where one would think lustre and delicacy out of place, the manufacturers continue to lavish gilding and polished steel to such an extent, that one is almost surprised at the

housemaid's daring to light a fire upstairs at all.
Of course the fire-irons are made to match, and it
is a positive fact that in some houses each drawing-
room fireplace has two pokers—a humble one for
actual use, and the other, of burnished steel, kept
simply to look at! It is needless to say, that while
such absurd practices as these continue, we can hardly
hope for a healthy and vigorous development of what
may be called household art. If fire-irons are used
at all, they should be made of a material which justifies their real purpose. The upper portions may be
of polished steel, though even this seems a needless refinement; but the rest should be of iron, and as simple
as possible in design. ' Berlin black' is the best sort
of lacquer for stoves and fenders, if in summer-time
they are required to look fresh and new. ' Blacklead'
is a modern abomination, which should be very sparingly used. With regard to ornament, it should be
borne in mind that incised patterns, however rudely
executed, are much more effective than heavy mouldings. The last we feel almost instinctively to be out
of place in solid metal-work. Of course, in the design
of small objects executed in brass and the more precious metals, the case is different, for they are seen
nearer the eye, and are for the most part made by

hand from thin plates of the material used; but a complexity of *cast* mouldings is the most uninteresting mode of decoration which could be devised for grates and fenders.

Italian ironwork of the fourteenth and fifteenth centuries was often decorated with incised and punctured patterns. The town of Siena abounds in instances of this mode of decoration, which may be still seen on the rings, bolts, and torch-brackets of ordinary domestic use. The well-known examples in the streets of Florence are later in date and more florid in execution,

though still very beautiful. But the glories of ancient
iron and bronze-work are not confined to Italy. In
Nuremberg, during the early Renaissance period, this
art was practised by men who, like Peter Vischer,
have left lasting monuments of their skill in the shape
of fountains, shrines, &c. Indeed, much may be learnt
at home if we examine with attention the treasures of
metallic art which such churches as our own Westminster Abbey, and St. George's Chapel, Windsor,
contain—to say nothing of humbler specimens—locks,
hinges, grilles, &c., which may be met with in almost
every old town of England.

As an example of the ingenuity and spirit with
which the design of ancient metal-work was formerly
treated in the manufacture of common articles of household use, I give an illustration of a curious iron candlestick in the possession of Professor Brewer. It was
purchased in Switzerland, and was probably made in
that country. In mode of construction it is most workmanlike, while the details display great fertility of invention. The ornamental portions are composed of
small bars of iron beaten out flat at one end, and drawn
to a point at the other. The pointed ends are twisted
into a spiral form, and the flat ends are split into two
straps shaped like volutes, the whole being put together

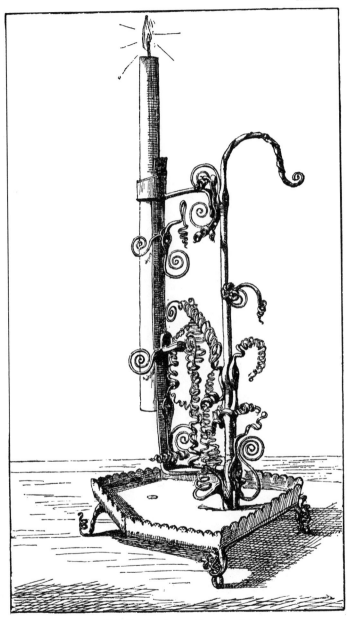

XXII

Old Swiss Iron Candlestick,
in the possession of Professor Brewer.

with iron pins. This mode of treating ironwork is exceedingly suggestive, and so simple in character that it might be easily adopted by any village blacksmith. The candlestick stands about eighteen inches high. Its date can hardly be identified, but it is probably not later than the seventeenth century. At that period, no doubt, it answered its purpose very well; and although the reproduction of such an article now, in its original form, cannot be recommended from a practical point of view, there are in modern use many objects of decorative metal-work, which might be successfully treated with the same spirit of design, if ever a time should arrive when the British workman becomes less of a machine and more of an artist, in the exercise of his handicraft.

It is, in fact, with the products of modern manufacture that we have now chiefly to deal; and here I cannot help expressing regret that, owing to the apathy of the public, an excellent step towards reform in this department of art has fallen so short of what was expected from it some few years ago.

Messrs. Hardman and Messrs. Hart were, I believe, among the first who endeavoured to revive the principles of good design in ecclesiastical metal-work and ironmongery—an example which has since been

followed by Messrs. Benham and Froud, and other
manufacturers, who have identified themselves with the
spécialité of domestic metal-work. The goods thus produced are infinitely superior to what is sold in the
ordinary way of trade. From the most elaborate church-
furniture down to the simplest article of domestic use,
the work is solid and well executed. Instead of the
vulgar cast-iron fenders and stove fittings which are
usually supplied for the domestic hearth, we have metal

which has been wrought or punched into its legitimate
form. The brass candlesticks and corona lamps, the
'closing-rings' and finger-plates, many of them treated
with great elegance of design, are stoutly made and
duly polished by machinery; whereas the meretricious
sheen which we see on ordinary ware is the result of
nothing but a coloured lacquer, which conceals the
natural hue of the brass beneath it.

It may be wondered why, with establishments of this kind in London, the British public go on buying such trashy articles as are usually offered at the general ironmongers'—the sprawling chandeliers, the photographic coal-boxes, and Louis Quinze clocks in ormolu, which once passed muster as 'tasteful.' But here a practical question presents itself. It is a choice not only between good or bad taste, but between bad taste which is cheap and good taste which is certainly somewhat dear. The manufacturers state they require a larger demand before they can lower their prices. The public say they must have more reasonable prices before they can afford to buy.

Meanwhile, an art from which much was expected at its late revival is not encouraged to the extent which it deserves. The examples which are produced for 'stock' year by year rarely improve in design. People have come to regard this modern *dinanderie* as something only fit for churches, or to suit the taste of young ladies whose ecclesiastical sentiment takes an æsthetic form. But, in point of fact, it ought to find its way into every household, and replace the absurdities which we have so long tolerated.

Chapter VI.

THE DRAWING-ROOM.

IN the field of taste, whether social or æsthetical, it is always much easier to point out paths which should be avoided than to indicate the road which leads to excellence. And although, while endeavouring to define the errors of bad art in its application to manufacture, it is easy to explain those principles which should guide the reader in appreciating good and sound design, there is some difficulty in illustrating such principles by familiar example. Thus, with regard to furniture, it was useless to direct attention to any one particular style of modern workmanship, while all styles were equally open to objection. The time, however, has at length come when more than one upholsterer has taken up the subject in an artistic spirit, and, instead of entrusting the design of his chairs and tables to the caprice of ignorant mechanics, whose notions of beauty are generally based on conventional ugliness, in remodelling his own taste by the study of ancient examples, or seeking the assistance of those who have received an art-education.

Meanwhile there will be a large majority of the public who cannot afford to buy furniture of the best class, but who are obliged to take whatever articles may be 'in fashion' at ordinary shops. Now there are degrees of excellence in all things, and as it is just possible some of these articles may be less objectionable than the rest, I venture to offer a few hints which may guide the inexperienced purchaser in choosing.

In the first place, never attach the least importance to any recommendation which (at such establishments) the shopman may make on the score of taste. If he says that one form of chair is *stronger* than another form, or that the covering of one sofa will wear better than that which is used for another, you may believe him, because on that point he can judge, and it is to his interest that you should be correctly informed so far. But on the subject of taste his opinion is not likely to be worth more, but rather less, than that of his customers, for the plain reason that the nature of his occupation can have left him little time to form a taste at all. He neither made the furniture in his shop nor superintended its design. His business is simply to sell it, and it will generally be found that his notions of beauty are kept subservient to this object. In other words, he will praise each article in turn, exactly as he considers your attention is attracted to it with a view to purchase. If he has any guiding principles of selection, they are chiefly based on two considerations—viz. the relative price of his goods, and the social position or wealth of those customers in whose eyes they find favour.

The public are frequently misled by terms of approbation now commonly used by shopmen in a sense widely remote from their original significance. Thus, the word 'handsome' has come to mean something which is generally showy, often ponderous, and almost always encumbered with superfluous ornament; the word 'elegant' is applied to any object which is curved in form (no matter in what direction, or with what effect). If it succeeds in conveying a false idea of its purpose, and possesses the additional advantage of being unlike anything that we have ever seen before, it is not only 'elegant' but 'unique.' If an article is of simple and good design, answering its purpose without ostentatious display of ornament, and pretending to be neither more nor less than it is, the ordinary furniture salesmen only call it 'neat.' I will not go so far as to recommend every 'neat' article of household use which may be displayed for sale, but I strongly advise my readers to refrain from buying any article of art-manufacture which is 'handsome,' 'elegant,' or 'unique,' in commercial slang : it is sure to be bad art.

The best and most picturesque furniture of all ages has been simple in general form. It may have been enriched by complex details of carved-work or inlay, but its main outlay was always chaste and sober in design, never running into extravagant contour or unnecessary curves. Anyone who will take the trouble to examine the few specimens of Egyptian furniture which are to be seen in the British Museum, the illustrations of ancient Greek and Roman art which have been published, or the mediæval examples which still exist in many an old sacristy abroad, and in most of our English country mansions, cannot fail to be struck with two qualities which distinguish this early handiwork from our own, viz. solidity and simplicity of construction.

The sofa at Knole, which dates from the same period as the chair which I have already described, is an example of thoroughly good design in its class. In the first place, its general shape is rectangular, clearly indi-

cating the construction of its wooden framework, the
joints of which are properly 'tenoned' and pinned
together in such a manner as to ensure its constant
stability. The back is formed like that of the chair,
with a horizontal rail only at its upper edge, but receives
additional strength from the second rail, which is
introduced at the back of the seat. By means of an
iron rack attached to each end, the sides can be raised
or lowered to any angle, thus enabling the sofa to be
used as a couch or a settee, at pleasure. These moveable sides, like the back, are stuffed with feathers,
while the seat itself is provided with two ample
cushions of the same material. A more luxurious
form of couch—to say nothing of the richness and elegance of its external covering—could hardly have been
devised, and yet there is not a single curve in its outline.
After 250 years of use, this sofa is still *comfortable*,
and, with the exception that the velvet and trimmings
are necessarily faded with age, remains in excellent
preservation. It was introduced by Mr. Marcus Stone
in his very clever picture of the 'Stolen Keys,' which
some of my readers may remember at the Royal
Academy Exhibition. Can we suppose that in the
year of Grace 2100 any English artist of taste will be
found willing to paint the 'elegant' *fauteuils* with

XXIII

Ancient Sofa,

in the Long Gallery, Knole.

which some English ladies still furnish their drawing-rooms ? And if such a painter is forthcoming, where will he find such an object to depict ? Possibly in some 'Chamber of Horrors' which may be devised at the South Kensington Museum to illustrate the progress of bad taste in this century, but rarely in any private house. It is hardly too much to say that fifty years hence most of our early 'Victorian' upholstery will have fallen into useless lumber, only fit to be burnt for firewood.

There is a notion very prevalent among people who have given themselves but little trouble to think at all on the matter, that to ensure grace in furniture, it must be made in a flimsy and fragile manner. Thus we constantly hear the expression '*light* and elegant' applied to a set of drawing-room chairs which look as if they must sink beneath the weight of the first middle-aged gentleman who used them. Now, lightness and elegance are agreeable qualities in their way, and, under certain conditions of design, should be aimed at. For instance, the treatment of mere surface ornament, such as painted arabesques, &c., or of details purely decorative and useless, as the filagree gold of a lady's earring, may well be of this character ; but objects intended for real and daily service, such as a table

which has to bear the weight of heavy books or dishes,
or a sofa on which we may recline at full length, ought
not to look light and elegant, but strong and comely;
for comeliness, whether in nature or art, is by no means
incompatible with strength. The Roman gladiator
had a grace of his own, but it was not the grace of
Antinous. Our modern furniture is essentially effeminate in form. How often do we see in fashionable
drawing-rooms a type of couch which seems to be composed of nothing but cushions! It is really supported
by a framework of wood or iron, but this internal
structure is carefully concealed by the stuffing and
material with which the whole is covered. I do not
wish to be ungallant in my remarks, but I fear there is
a large class of young ladies who look upon this sort of
furniture as 'elegant.' Now, if elegance means nothing
more than a milliner's idea of the beautiful, which
changes every season—so that a bonnet which is pronounced 'lovely' in 1877 becomes a 'fright' in 1878—
then no doubt this sofa, as well as a score of other
articles of modern manufacture which I could mention,
is elegant indeed. But, if elegance has anything in
common with real beauty—beauty which can be estimated by a fixed and lasting standard—then I venture
to submit that this eccentric combination of bad car-

pentry and bloated pillows is very *in*elegant, and, in fact, a piece of ugliness which we ought not to tolerate in our houses.

Most of us, who know anything of country life, have seen the common wooden settle which forms so comfortable and snug-looking a seat by rustic hearths. No artist who ever studied the interior of a cottage would hesitate to introduce so picturesque an object in his sketch. But imagine such a sofa as I have described, in a view of the most magnificent and chastely-decorated chamber in Europe, and it would at once appear commonplace and uninteresting. Perhaps my readers may feel inclined to urge that a great deal of the interest with which we are accustomed to regard old rustic furniture is due to its age and dilapidation. It may be so; but can we expect or believe that a modern chair or couch, as they were lately manufactured, will ever, by increasing years, attain the dignified appearance of Tudor or Jacobean furniture? The truth is that such household gods become dingy under our very eyes, and the very best of them will not survive the present generation.

Now it is by no means advisable that we should fit up our drawing-rooms with cottage settles, or adopt any sort of furniture which is not perfectly consistent

with ordinary notions of comfort and convenience.   If
our social habits differ from those of our forefathers,
the fittings of our rooms must follow suit.   But, in
point of fact, there is a great deal of ignorant prejudice
on these points.   We all know, for instance, that the
old low-seated chair, with its high padded back (commonly called Elizabethan), is considered awkward and
uncomfortable, simply because its proportions are
strange to us.   We know, too, that the ' occasional '
chair of modern drawing-rooms, with a moulded bar,
and perhaps a knot of carving, which chafes our
shoulder blades as we lean back upon it, is looked on
as an article of refined luxury.   As to the comparative
merit of their respective designs, from an artistic point
of view, there can be but little question; but if any of
my readers have any doubt which is the more comfortable, I would strongly advise them to try each, after a
fatiguing walk.   Perhaps they will find that the art of
chair-making has not improved to such an extent as
they imagine since the days of good Queen Bess.   But,
however much opinion may vary on this point, one
thing remains certain—viz., that beauty of form may
be perfectly compatible with strength of material, and
that good design can accommodate itself to the most
fastidious notions of convenience.

The annexed woodcuts, representing drawing-room chairs manufactured by Messrs. Jackson and Graham, show how easily a few incised patterns and turned

mouldings may be substituted for the lumpy carving and 'shaped' legs usually found in such furniture.

A familiar and apparently very obvious distinction has been made, from time immemorial, between the useful and the ornamental, as if the abstract qualities represented by these words were completely independent of each other. It would, however, be a shortsighted philosophy which failed to recognise, even in a moral sense, many points of contact between the two.

If that which pleases the eye—if that which charms the ear—if that which appeals to the more imaginative faculties of the human mind have no direct and practical result for our benefit, then poets, painters, and musicians have, indeed, lived and wrought for

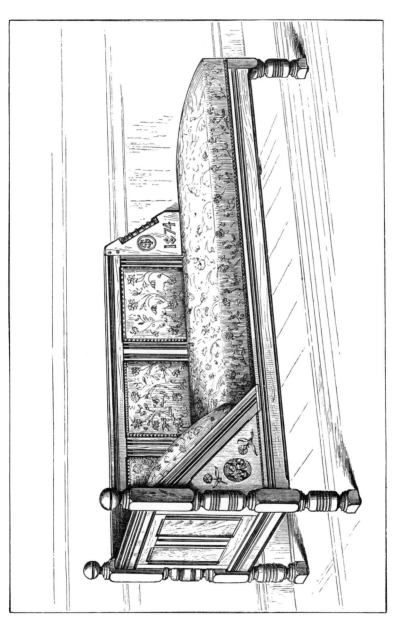

XXIV

Drawing-Room Sofa,

executed by Jackson & Graham from a design by Charles L. Eastlake.

us in vain. And if, on the other hand, we are unable to perceive, even in the common concerns and practical details of daily toil—in the merchant's calling, in the blacksmith's forge, and in the chemist's laboratory —the romantic side of life's modern aspect, it must be but a weakly order of sentiment with which we are inspired by songs and books and pictures.

In the sphere of what is called industrial art, use and beauty are, in theory at least, closely associated : for not only has the humblest article of manufacture, when honestly designed, a picturesque interest of its own, but no decorative feature can legitimately claim our admiration without revealing by its very nature the purpose of the object which it adorns. Yet, among half-educated minds, nothing is more common than to retain two distinct and utterly opposed ideals of beauty —one of a poetic and sentimental kind, which leads people to prefer certain conditions of form and colour in pictorial representations of 'still life'; and the other of a conventional and worldly kind, through which we not only tolerate, but approve, the dubious 'elegancies' of fashionable upholstery. Let us suppose, for example, a young lady, of average taste and intelligence, suddenly called upon to sketch some familiar article of household use for her drawing-master. She would

surely rather choose the housemaid's bucket or an
Italian oil-flask for a subject, than her own work-table ;
and she would be right.   Yet, if she were asked to say
candidly which she considered the *prettiest* of the three,
her decision would probably be in favour of the work-
table—and she would be wrong.   For if there be any
true principles of design at all, no article of manufac-

ture can be rightly called 'pretty' in which those principles are violated.   Buckets and oil-flasks, we all
know, are plain articles of honest handicraft, pretending
to be neither more nor less than what they are.   If
we examine one of the former, we shall find it constructed of oak, or some other tough wood, cut into
narrow strips or staves, from three to four inches wide,
and about half an inch thick.   These staves are arranged
concentrically, edge to edge, and gradually diminish in

width downwards, because the bucket, for convenience
of use as well as of manufacture, is made smaller at its
lower end.   They are held together by strong bands
of hoop-iron, which are slipped over the lower and
smaller diameter of the bucket, and driven back as far
as they will go towards the larger diameter.   This
makes a tighter cincture than it would be possible to
ensure by any other means. The staves have previously
been grooved on their inner side to receive the bottom
of the bucket, which is a circular and generally solid
disc of wood.   In order to save the latter from wear,
it is inserted an inch or so higher than the bottom
edge of the staves ; and because buckets have frequently to be set down in sloppy places, three of the
staves are allowed to project a trifle longer than the
rest, so that in washing a floor or pavement the water
may flow underneath the bottom of the bucket.   The
bucket-staves are rounded at their upper end, in order
that there may be no sharp edge to injure the fingers.
The handle is a bow of wrought iron twisted into a
hook at each end, and thus attached to iron staple-rings
which are nailed at opposite sides of the bucket.   The
handle is expressly hammered wider and convex in
section just at its centre, in order that a hand may
grasp it with ease.

Now, the cooper who made this bucket had no more
notion of high art than of the Binomial Theorem.   He
merely adopted a type which has been in use, perhaps
for centuries, and is at once the most convenient and
comely in form which could have been invented for
the purpose.   Luckily, buckets are common articles
of English manufacture, costing so little that it is not
worth while to cheapen them further by inferior workmanship.   They are, moreover, used for purposes
too homely to need ' elegance ' of contour.   The consequence is, that they are simply sound in design and
construction.

Now let us look at the Florence flask, and note how
admirably both its shape and material are fitted for
their purpose.   Glass is an extremely
ductile substance, capable of being
blown and twisted into an endless
variety of forms.   But this bottle is
intended to contain olive-oil, an article
of common consumption in every
Italian household.   It must, therefore,
be cheaply and lightly made, but
strongly enough to be handled freely,
and hung up when not in use on the
nearest nail of a kitchen-wall.   The oval outline, there-

fore, which the flask assumes at its lower and more bulky end, is precisely the strongest which could have been invented for the material. It is the very form which Nature adopts for the purpose of holding a denser fluid in a more fragile vessel. But even eggs require to be packed carefully in straw for market; moreover they will not stand on end, nor are we able to pour out their contents without breaking the shell. So the Tuscan bottle-makers ingeniously set to work to meet those requirements for their flask. They pull out its upper end into a long narrow neck, which serves both as a duct and a handle. They twist a cord of dried grass in rings round the bulbous part of the bottle, and make them fast by three or four broad straps of the same material stretching longitudinally from top to bottom so as to form a complete and effective suit of straw armour. Finally, they continue the spiral cord downwards and outwards at the foot of the bottle, so as to form a little base for it to stand on, and they finish the cord upwards in a long twisted loop, which is just the thing to hang it up by. Thus, it will be seen that besides being an exceedingly picturesque object (for in the whole range of common ware it would be difficult to find a prettier one), this Florence flask is constructed on as sound and practical principles as the strictest utilitarian could wish.

But the modern English work-table, or any similar article of manufacture designed for fashionable households, is sure to belie its purpose in some way. It will probably have doors which look like drawers, or drawers which assume an appearance of doors. It will shroud up part of its wooden framing with silken plaits fringed with straight bands of gimp, and decorated at each angle with lumpy little tassels. It will be made of deal and veneered with walnut and mahogany. It will be 'enriched' with fictitious carving, and plastered over with delusive varnish.

Real art has no recourse to such tricks as these. It can accommodate itself to the simplest and most practical shapes which the carpenter or potter has invented, as well as to the most delicate and subtle forms of refined manufacture. There is no limit to the height of dignity which it can reach; there is no level of usefulness to which it will not stoop. You may have a good school of design for the art-workman : you may have a bad school of design for the art-workman; but you can have no *grand* school, for both the blacksmith and the goldsmith are bound by æsthetic laws of equal importance, and the same spirit which guides the chisel must direct the lathe.

In order to rightly estimate the artistic value and

fitness of that superfluous detail which is called ornament, we should first ask ourselves whether it indicates
by its general character the material which it enriches,
or of which it is itself composed.   If it does not, we
may fairly question the fitness of such ornament; but
if it suggests the idea of a different material, we may
be sure it is bad.   To a certain extent this principle
is admitted by people of ordinary taste.   No householder would think of allowing the panels of his
cabinet to be painted like an Indian shawl, however
beautiful the pattern on it might be.   Nor would he
tolerate a tablecloth of which the ornament was disposed in the form of door-panels.   But his dislike to
such examples of misapplied design would arise from
no deep-seated convictions on the subject; he would
simply object to see a mode of decoration adopted
for which he remembered no precedent.   Show the
same man a pink landscape at the bottom of a washing-
basin or a piece of bed-furniture printed in imitation of
carved scroll-work, and, just because he has been accustomed to see such things all his life, they seem right
and proper in his eyes.   Yet it is not a whit worse to
give wood the appearance of textile fabric than to let
chintz be stained and shaded like solid wood; nor is
our supposititious tablecloth at all inferior in design to

the pictorial absurdities which, not many years ago, we embodied in our crockery.

There is a general impression prevalent among people who are interested in the subject of art manufacture, that well-designed furniture must necessarily be expensive. The upholsterers themselves were once inclined to foster this notion, and whenever they brought out a new type of chair or cabinet which had any pretence to originality or excellence of form, they were sure to charge highly for it, because it was a novelty.

Now it may, indeed, happen that what are called 'fancy' articles, being made with a view to attract the notice of individual customers, cost more than those intended for general sale, because the former are manufactured in small quantities at a time, whereas the latter are produced in wholesale lots. But it is hard that the public should have to pay for a commercial mistake due to the apathy of tradesmen. Good artistic furniture ought really to be quite as cheap as that which is ugly. Every wretched knot of carving, every twist in the outline of a modern sofa, every bead and hollow executed in the turner's wheel has been the result of *design* in some form or another. The draughtsman and mechanic must be paid, whatever the nature of their tastes may be ; and no doubt as much thought, labour, and expense of material are bestowed on modern upholstery as would be necessary to ensure (under proper supervision) the highest qualities of which the cabinetmaker's art is capable.

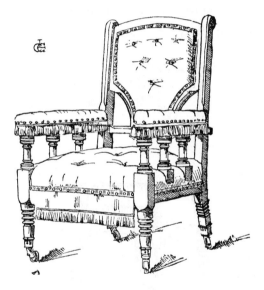

The drawing-room chairs of which illustrations are here given were made from my design at a price which certainly did not exceed what would have been charged for such articles at any respectable shop. I can at least testify to the excellence of their manufacture. They were constructed of oak, covered with velvet, and trimmed with silk fringe.

The truth is that even bad ornament is costly; and as there is a great deal of bad ornament in modern work, it is far better, while the present state of things continues, to choose the very plainest and simplest forms of domestic furniture procurable. These will, at least, be in better taste than the elaborate deformities by which they are surrounded. That they are

not always cheaper may be judged from the following anecdote: Some years ago, a gentleman observed at one of the furnishing warehouses a light cane-seated chair of a very ordinary description, but the design of which, with the exception of a certain bit of ornamental carving, pleased him. He inquired the price, and was told, thirty shillings.

' And what would it cost if that ornament were omitted ? ' he asked.

' Thirty-five shillings,' was the answer.

Here we have a crown extra charged for the superior intelligence required from a British workman—simply to *omit* a portion of his labour. This affords some clue to the extraordinary stagnation of art-impulses which, until lately, existed in this branch of manufacture. A certain shape was fixed upon—no one knew why—for the rail or leg of a chair, and, once executed, was multiplied indefinitely—whether by hand or by machinery it matters little. It was made, as it were, by *rote*, and doubtless contracted for at per gross. It would be absurd to expect furniture made in this way to possess any great refinement of design. But in general form, at least, it might be picturesque and sturdy, and these were just the qualities overlooked by modern cabinetmakers and joiners in their work, which—unless competent supervision be exercised—is generally frail and uninteresting.

I suppose that ever since the days of King Arthur, round tables have been in favour with knights and ladies. But the round table of mediæval carpentry was not the rickety, ill-contrived article which is manufactured now. The present system of balancing, by means of pins and screws, a circular framework of wood on a hollow boxed-up cylinder, is manifestly wrong in principle, for, in nine cases out of ten, tables made on this plan become unsteady and out of order after a few years' wear.   To obviate this evil the central leg or

stem should be made *solid*, with a base heavy and substantial enough to keep the table steady by its mere weight.   Four struts should then be introduced, stretching diagonally from the side of the stem to 'ledges,' screwed on the under surface of the circular top, which may be a simple disc of wood, about an inch in thickness; by this means the unsightly and   expensive mode of *framing* the table-top round its outer edge is rendered unnecessary, and that inconvenient tripod, which is always in the way of one's feet, may be avoided, while the whole table can be taken to pieces, when occasion requires, just as readily as those in ordinary use.

On the last page is a sketch of an old German table well adapted for cards or chess in a modern drawing-room. It may look inconvenient, but it really is not so, for the top considerably overhangs the framework below, and thus gives ample room to sitters.

The natural grain of such woods as oak, rosewood, walnut, &c., is in itself an ornamental feature, if it be not obscured and clogged by artificial varnish. But where an effect of greater richness is aimed at, two legitimate modes of decoration are available for wood, viz, carving and marquetry or inlaid work. For cabinets, coffers, sideboards, and other repositories of household goods, the wood-carver's art has been successfully employed in the best ages of design ; but it should be sparingly used for chairs, tables, couches, and in all situations where a knotted lump of wood is likely to prove inconvenient to the touch. It is a pity that marquetry should have fallen into such disuse, for it is a very effective and not necessarily expensive mode

of ornament.   It consists of inlaying the surface of one
wood with small pieces of another, differing from it in
vein or colour.   These pieces may either be grouped

in geometrical pattern, or arranged so as to represent
natural objects conventionally.   The *tarsia*, or old
Italian marquetry, was used for both purposes, and,

owing to the minute size of the inlaid pieces, was equally adapted for either. The sketch above is from an early Italian casket in the South Kensington Museum. The lower portion is of carved ivory, the lid being composed of ebony and ivory inlaid. It is probably of fourteenth-century manufacture. A somewhat similar specimen is given in M. Viollet le Duc's 'Dictionnaire du Mobilier Français.' But during the best and early period of the art, figures and animals, whenever thus portrayed, were treated in a formal and purely decorative manner. Some excellent examples of this sort occur in the cathedral stalls at Orvieto, in Italy. Two other kinds of inlay are well known in England—viz., that which prevailed on the Continent during the last century, and modern Indian work. Many specimens of the former are to be met with at the curiosity shops, and indeed are still reproduced and imported in large quantities from Holland. In this the inlaid pieces are larger, and frequently stained in imitation of fruit and flowers. The Indian Mosaics, being excessively minute, are well adapted for small objects, and frequently form the decoration of ivory caskets, workboxes, and even fans.

The small demand for *marquetry* at the present time has, of course, limited its production, and thus increased its cost in this country.   But, even if it should ever become popular, there will always remain a large proportion of household articles, especially in the upper storeys of an English house, where its use would be considered extravagant.   Indeed, it is quite possible for furniture to be well designed, independently of this or any other mode of surface decoration ; and it cannot be too frequently urged that simplicity of general form is one of the first conditions of artistic excellence in manufacture.   Many upholsterers now sell bed-room wardrobes, toilet-tables, &c., which (I suppose, from their extreme plainness of construction) are called *mediæval*.   They are executed in oak and stained deal, and are certainly a great improvement on the old designs in mahogany.   But, instead of being cheaper, as would be the case if they were made by the hundred and supplied to the 'general public,' they are often dearer than their more ornate and pretentious predecessors. The taste, no doubt, requires to be popularised to render it profitable to trade ; but whether it will ever become popular while people can buy more showy articles at a less price, may be questioned.

XXV

Drawing-Room Cheffonier,
executed by Jackson & Graham from a design by Charles L. Eastlake.

Chapter VII.

WALL-FURNITURE.

HAVING already considered the subject of paper-hangings, I will now offer a few hints on what may be called the *wall-furniture* of rooms in general, and of the drawing-room in particular. In most houses the chief example of this class is the mantel-piece mirror. Custom and convenience have long since determined its position, and, considering the nature of our social habits in this country, and the importance which we attach to a fireside in almost every apartment, one can scarcely doubt that, if a glass is to be fixed anywhere on the internal walls of a modern house, this is the place for it. Unfortunately, however, while it gives apparent size and real brightness to a room, it is a feature which, as ordinarily designed, is in itself eminently uninteresting. The mere fact that it presents to the eye a reflection of every object in front of its plane is of course not sufficient to make it decora-

tive. Accordingly we find it enclosed in a gilt frame,
or, to speak more correctly, a wooden frame plastered
over with composition to imitate carving of a most
extravagant kind, and then gilded—a bad style of
work, even if the design were tolerable.   But it is
usually in the worst taste. Now old frames made in
the last and previous centuries, whatever their style may
have been, had at least this advantage, that they were
moulded and carved out of solid wood, and the difference between them and those of modern manufacture
is scarcely less than the difference between well-
modelled statuettes and the common plaster-casts which
are sold by an itinerant image-man.   We should be
ashamed to place the latter on our mantel-pieces. Why
are we to tolerate in one class of decorative art the
vulgarities which we despise in another ?   If real
carved work cannot be afforded, it is far better to let
such mirrors be fitted in plain solid frames of wood,
say three or four inches in width, enriched with delicate
mouldings or incised ornament.   If executed in oak,
they may be left of their natural colour : if in the
commoner kind of wood, they can be ebonised (i.e.
stained black), and further decorated with gold in incised surface patterns or delicate mouldings.   This
ought to be a less expensive, as it certainly would be

a more effective, process than that of gilding the entire surface.

But we have other examples of wall-furniture to consider. The practice of hanging up oil and water-colour paintings, engravings, and photographs in our sitting-rooms, is one which I need scarcely say contributes greatly to that appearance of comfort which is the especial characteristic of an English house. And it can do more than this. Independently of the intrinsic value which such works of art may possess, they become collectively an admirable means of legitimate decoration. Assuming, then, that the prints and pictures we wish to hang are of some artistic interest, the question arises how we can dispose them on our walls to the best advantage. Success in this respect will mainly depend on two points, viz., their judicious association, and the design of frames. The first step should be to *classify.* Oil-paintings should, if possible, be kept in a room by themselves. The force of their colour is always greater than that which can be attained by other 'vehicles,' and will therefore, in juxtaposition with water-colour drawings, make the latter look poor and feeble in effect. It is an old English custom to hang family portraits in the dining-room, and it seems a reasonable custom. Generally large in size, and enclosed in massive frames, they appear well suited to an apartment which experience has led us to furnish in a more solid and substantial manner than any other in the house. Besides, the Dining-room is especially devoted to hospitality and family gatherings, and it is pleasant on such occasions to be surrounded by mementos of those who once, perhaps, formed members of a social circle which they have long ceased to join. But where such portraits are few in number, there can be no objection to add to this group such other oil pictures as may be in the house, unless they are sufficiently numerous to fill another room by themselves.

Of course, by filling a room I do not mean crowding its walls almost from the wainscot to the ceiling—a practice which, so long as there is a convenient space elsewhere, is much to be avoided. In annual public exhibitions, the enormous number of works sent for display frequently renders it necessary to hang them three or four deep on the walls ; but in the rooms of an ordinary private house there is no necessity for such an arrangement. To see pictures with anything like comfort or attention, they should be disposed in one row only, and that opposite the eye, or on an average about 5 feet 6 inches from the floor to the centre of the canvas. (I refer now to ordinary-sized pictures; of course, full-length portraits of life-size and other large works require to be hung higher.) A row thus formed will make a sort of coloured zone around the room, and though the frames themselves may vary

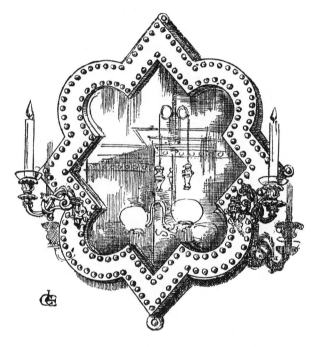

in shape and dimensions, they can generally be grouped with something like symmetry of position, the larger ones being kept in the centre, and the smaller ones being ranged on either side in corresponding places along the line.

It is, however, by no means necessary to good effect that the drawings or paintings thus arranged should come into close contact. On the contrary, it is often a much better plan to separate them, especially in a drawing-room, by such small objects as sconces, small ornamental mirrors, or little wooden brackets, support-ing statuettes, vases, &c. There is a very pretty form of mirror, probably Venetian in its origin, which has lately been manufactured at a trifling cost, and may be used for this purpose. The general form of the frame is that of a lozenge intersected by a quatrefoil. It is made of wood, covered with coloured velvet, and studded at its edges with nails, which may be either gilt or silvered.

Small wooden brackets, in great variety of shape, can of course be bought at any ordinary upholsterer's, but as a rule they are weak in construction and of very inferior design. The pierced open-work with which their lower portions are usually decorated would be a perfectly legitimate means of ornamentation for such objects, if properly introduced ; but in this, as in all cases where wood-work is thus treated, the pattern should be represented by the portion cut away, and not by that which is left. The following example, though of a very simple shape, will suffice to illustrate

my meaning. It is hardly necessary to add that the
so called 'ornamental' leather-work which a few years
ago was so in vogue with young ladies, who used it for

the construction of brackets, baskets, picture-frames,
&c., was—like potichomanie, diaphanie, and other
modern drawing-room pursuits—utterly opposed to
sound principles of taste. Pieces of leather cut into

the shape of leaves and flowers, glued together and varnished, represent at best but a wretched parody of the carver's art.   The characteristic beauty of oriental china and of painted windows can never be even suggested by bits of coloured paper gummed to the surface of glass.   Such work as this may be the rage for a few seasons, but sooner or later must fall, as it deserves to fall, into universal contempt.

The art of picture-hanging requires much nicety and no little patience, for it is difficult to measure distances between the *centres* of frames along a wall.   One method of getting over the difficulty is to have an iron or brass rod fixed at the top of the wall, just under the ceiling, and fitted with sliding rings, to which the pictures may be attached by wire or cord.   But this plan involves some expense, and it is hardly worth while to adopt it for ordinary use.   Picture-rings are generally fixed at the back of the frame, and some inches below its upper edge; this throws the picture forward at the top, which some people consider an advantage.   But this inclination, though sometimes desirable in the highest row of a crowded gallery, is useless when every picture is hung 'on the line.' Moreover, a light frame thus suspended is never steady, but liable to rock with the slightest motion.   A better plan is to screw the rings on the *upper edge* of the frame, which will then lie flat against the wall. When nails are used for picture-hanging, they should be driven into the wall just under the bottom line of the cornice, and, for obvious reasons, never lower down on the wall, where it can possibly be avoided. As, however, internal walls, or those which separate room from room, or rooms from passages, are often merely framed partitions, filled in with lath and plaster, it is not always easy to find a holdfast for the nail; but, by gently tapping the wall with a hammer, it is easy to find where the solid wood—or, as the carpenters call it, the 'stud'—occurs, and there the nail will hold fast enough.

A framed picture, however small, should never be suspended from *one* nail. This may seem a trifle; but, for the sake of appearance as well as of safety, it is better to depend on two points of support. The triangular space enclosed by a picture-cord stretched between three points must always be inharmonious with the horizontal and vertical lines of a room.

If it is desirable, as I have said, to hang oil pictures by themselves, it is doubly advisable to separate water-colour drawings and photographs or engravings. Each may be beautiful in their way, but to place them together is to destroy the effect of both. The print

will look cold and harsh by the side of the water-colour
sketch; the sketch will seem unreal and gaudy by the
side of the photograph.   Keep them all apart—if not
in separate rooms, at least on separate walls.   Never
hang glazed drawings, where it can be avoided, opposite a window.   The sheen of the glass reflects the
daylight, and destroys the effect of the picture behind
it.   Take care that your picture-cord either matches or
harmonises with the colour of the wall-paper behind it.
Sometimes wire, which is almost invisible at a little
distance, is used instead of cord.   The real advantage
of wire is that it does not harbour dust, but it is not so
easily adjusted or altered in its length as cord.*

Thus much for the hanging of pictures.   On the
subject of frames themselves, much might be said.   I
have endeavoured to show that the only proper means
of arriving at correct form in objects of decorative
art is to bear in mind the practical purpose to which
such objects will be applied.   Now the use of a
picture-frame is obvious.   It has to give additional
strength to the light 'strainer' of wood over which
paper or canvas is stretched.   It may also have to
hold glass securely over the picture.   Lastly, it has

---

* There is a recent invention called 'wire-cord,' in which both materials are incorporated.

XXVI

Picture Frame Mouldings,
designed by E. J. Tarver.

on its outer face to form a border which, while ornamental in itself, shall tend, by dividing the picture
from surrounding objects, to confine the eye of the
spectator within its limits. These conditions seem
simple enough, but how frequently are they violated
in modern work! The outer frame, instead of being
made of oak or some other tough wood, is too
frequently constructed of deal strips lightly glued
together. In place of carving, the wood is overlaid
with a species of composition moulded into wretched
forms, which pass for ornament as soon as they are
gilded. These are so brittle that, instead of protecting the picture, they have to be handled more carefully than the glass itself, and are liable to chip at the
slightest blow. Finally, instead of confining attention
to the picture, this sort of frame distracts the eye by
its fussiness. Now, gilding on a picture-frame is not
only justifiable by way of ornament, but is much to be
recommended as a foil or neutral ground for enhancing
the value of colour; but it ought to be laid directly
on the wood, without any intervening composition ;
and if any ornament in relief is attempted, it should
be carved in the solid material. The effect of oak-
grain seen through leaf-gold is exceedingly good, and
the appearance of *texture* thus produced is infinitely

more interesting than the smooth monotony of gilt 'compo.'

This, however, is a point which the ordinary and uneducated professional decorator will generally dispute. When I look into the windows of some establishments devoted to decorative art, and see the monstrosities which are daily offered to the public in the name of taste—the fat gilt cupids, the coarse and clumsy mouldings, the heavy plaster cornices, and the lifeless types of leaves and flowers which pass for ornament in the nineteenth century—I cannot help thinking how much we might learn from those nations whose art it has long been our custom to despise—from the half-civilised craftsmen of Japan, and the rude barbarians of Feejee.

It is a practice with many artists of the rising English school to design their own frames for the pictures which they exhibit, and some excellent specimens may now and then be seen on the walls of the Royal Academy,* and at the Old Water-Colour Society's Rooms. Coloured sketches which are surrounded by a wide margin of white paper will look well in plain, ungilded oak frames. When, for economy's sake, deal is used,

---

* Those enclosing the pictures of Mr. F. Leighton, R.A., and, I believe, designed by the artist himself, may be mentioned as good examples.

it may be painted, and parcel-gilt black frames are
often very effective. I have seen some painted white,
which are suitable for engravings. Indeed, both for
engravings and photographs, gilt frames seem to
be out of place. Wherever paint is used, it should

be well flatted, so as not to shine. Heavy mouldings, except for a large frame, are to be avoided.
Whenever they are introduced, they should slope back
from the surface of the picture towards the wall behind,
and not forward, so as to throw a shadow on the picture. As a rule, for water-colour drawings of an ordinary size, a plain frame, with a few delicate mouldings
or a mere chamfered edge, will be all-sufficient. If en-

richment is desired, it is better and less expensive to *incise* ornament than to carve it in relief, and it will be found more effective to stop the mouldings or chamfering a few inches short of the end on each side. This will leave an angle block at each corner, forming good points for incised decoration.

Some years ago a new type of light oaken frame, commonly called *cruciform*, was introduced, and for a time became very popular; but one is apt to become wearied of a form that is seen everywhere, without the least variety of proportion; and there is a poor, wiry look about the thinnest of the cruciform frames which is unsatisfactory. If artists of note would steadily refuse to adopt the commonplace inventions of the ordinary frame-maker, and, taking a few hints from old examples, would get their own designs executed, there might be some hope of reform in this direction.

Frames made for engravings can scarcely be too simple in design, and when two or three prints of the same size and general character have to be hung in one room, it is well to group them side by side in one long frame divided into compartments by a light fillet or beading. On the following page is the sketch of a frame arranged on this principle. The best woodcuts of the present day are perhaps the most desirable examples of modern art which can be possessed at a trifling cost. Chromo-lithographs are, of course, much more attractive to the public, and are popularly supposed to be a cheap and easy method of encouraging pictorial taste; but, with a few rare exceptions, they do more harm than good in this respect. In the representation of purely decorative art, where the beauty of design

depends chiefly upon grace of outline, and upon association, rather than gradation or blending of tints, chromo-lithography may do good service; but in the field of landscape art, for which this invention has been chiefly employed, it is in a two-fold way worse than useless. In the first place it accustoms the eye to easily-rendered and therefore *tricky* effects of colour which falsify rather than illustrate nature. Secondly, it encourages a flimsy style of water-colour painting which

no true artist would adopt but with a view of render-
ing his picture easy to be thus imitated. A draughtsman's handiwork in the delineation of form and in the
distribution of light and shade may, indeed, under
certain conditions, be reproduced by mechanical means,
but the subtle delicacies of colour in good pictorial art
are utterly unapproachable in a print which attempts
to render, with a few super-imposed tints, the dexterity
and refinement of manual skill.   Original works of art,
whether in oil or water-colours, are only within reach
of the wealthy. But photographs and good wood-
engravings are procurable at a moderate cost, and are
far more serviceable than chromo-lithography in the
development of household taste.

Chapter VIII.

THE BED-ROOM.

T HE modern development of art is full of strange inconsistencies, and they are nowhere more apparent than in the connection of design with manufacture. Many people who are fully alive to the inartistic character of the furniture with which they surround themselves, and who would gladly hail a reform in upholstery, are deterred from helping to forward that movement by a fear that, if they did so, their chairs and tables would not be what is called 'in keeping' with the house which they inhabit. This plea, however, for tolerating the present state of things, is worthless. It would be hard, indeed, if, because the builders and land-owners compel us to live in square ugly boxes of inferior brickwork, plastered over with a delusive mask of perishable stucco, we were on that account compelled to purchase furniture as mean, as fragile, or as pretentious as our ordinary town dwellings have become. And if we are to defer the consideration of household taste until we have remodelled our national architecture, we may wait for ever. Of late years there has, indeed, been much improvement in the design of our churches and some other public buildings, but the general aspect of London streets and suburban residences remains hopelessly uninteresting, and is likely to continue so while they lie at the mercy of speculating builders, and a system of tenure which gives the landlord but a temporary interest in the stability of his houses.

If the style of our architecture were definitely Italian, it would naturally become a question whether we should be justified in fitting up our homes with any class of furniture but that which prevailed during the Renaissance period. But while May-fair remains what it is, a dull labyrinth of bricks and mortar, it can afford no possible standard of uniformity for the design of the sofas and sideboards within its walls.

Yet the very people who believed in this undesirable consistency of ugliness, did not hesitate to furnish several rooms of a modern house, each after its own particular fashion, and no considerations of beauty or convenience were allowed to interfere with conventional notions of propriety. The consequence was that furniture in the last generation generally reminded

us less of its use than of trades connected with it. The
great solemn dining-room, with its heavy sarcopha-
gus-like sideboards and funereal window-curtains, was
eminently suggestive of the undertaker's calling.   Upstairs, the ormolu decoration, the veneered walnut
tables, the florescent carpet and sofa-cover recalled to
our memory the upholstering youth who so confidently
expressed his opinion on their merits.   And a storey
higher, somehow, in the midst of lace bed-curtains,
muslin toilet covers, pink calico, and cheval glasses,
one might fancy oneself in a milliner's shop.

Now all these rooms ought indeed to be furnished
characteristically of their purpose, but by no means in
various styles.   The wardrobe must, of necessity, be
different in shape from the cabinet, the bed from the
sofa, the wash-stand from the sideboard; but the
general *principle* of design in all these objects should
be the same.   The chair which can be pointed out as
a ' bed-room chair,' and the carpet which may be described particularly as a ' drawing-room carpet,' are
sure (under the ordinary system of design, at all
events) to be in bad taste.

As a rule, our modern bed-rooms are too *fussy* in
their fitting up. People continually associate the words
' luxurious and comfortable ' as if they were synony-

mous.   In reality they suggest two distinct aims which
should not be confounded.   Glaring chintzes, elaborate
wall-papers, French polish, and rich draperies on every
side, may represent considerable expense and a certain
order of luxury, but assuredly not comfort.

Now, one of the points on which it is necessary to
insist is this, that excellence of design may be, and,
indeed, frequently is, quite independent of cost.   I
might go further, and say with truth that the style of
inferior design is sure to deteriorate in proportion to its
richness.   Some of the worse specimens of decorative
art that one sees exposed for sale are expensive
articles of luxury.   Some of the most appropriately
formed, and therefore most artistic, objects of household
use are to be bought for a trifling sum.   Take the common bed-room wash-hand-stand, for instance, I mean
such a one as will be found in the upper bed-rooms
of a moderately-sized house.   It is made of deal or
birch wood, and usually painted, it must be confessed, after rather a ridiculous fashion—viz., in imitation of oak or bird's-eye maple.   But its shape is a
reasonable shape, and could hardly be improved.   It
is fitted with two shelves, the upper one cut to receive
the basin, and the lower one 'boxed' to receive a
drawer.   It has a splash-board to protect the wall

against which it is placed. It is supported on four legs turned and shaped after a fashion infinitely superior to that of an ordinary dining-table. It is not, indeed, an example of high art in manufacture, but it is an instance of honest workmanship, and until we get honest work, we can have no artistic furniture. Now observe, the form of this cheap and common washstand is good, because it happens to be traditional. The pattern has probably varied little ever since such articles were first used in England. It has never been worth while to alter the shape of a piece of furniture only used in second-rate bed-rooms, and which costs, say, from 40s. to 50s. But with articles of luxury it is different. Your 'superior Spanish mahogany washstand, with carved standards and marble top on castors,' may be of more valuable material than its humbler prototype, but in regard to design it is often not nearly so good. The marble top and sides, instead of being left plain, are 'shaped' into senseless curves. The four corner legs are often banished as too obvious and ordinary a means of support, and an attempt is made to balance the wash-stand on two mis-shapen lumps of wood called 'standards;' but as these would certainly be insecure in themselves, they are allowed to expand each into minor legs or claws towards the floor.

Finally, the whole of the wood-work (probably veneered) is covered with French polish, which looks
smart enough when first applied, but which gradually
grows shabby and shabbier with every drop of water
spilt upon it. The price of this 'superior' article is
from six to eight guineas.

It is absurd to suppose that such an enormous
disparity of cost between the third-floor and the
second-floor wash-stands can be accounted for simply
by a difference in the intrinsic value of their respective
materials. The truth is that a vast amount of money
is continually being wasted on bad art in the way of
carving, &c., which passes for elegance with the
million, but which all who are familiar with the conditions of good design must regard with contempt.
This mistake is not confined to bed-room floors. The
kitchen dresser, regarded from an artistic point of view,
is really more reasonable in form and more picturesque
than the dining-room sideboard ; the servants' coal-box
than the illuminated scuttle in my lady's boudoir ; and
so on throughout the house. It is not, of course, the
use of rich material alone, or the elaboration of ornament, but the misapplication of both, which leads to
error in art-manufacture. It would be extremely
absurd to use gold or silver in making a coal-box, yet

these metals, even in such a situation, would be as capable of artistic treatment as iron or copper. It would be the height of extravagance to construct a sideboard of cedar or sandal-wood, yet such materials

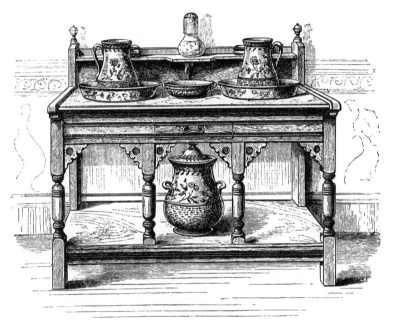

could be well adapted to the purpose. But papier-maché ornaments on a scuttle, or a *buffet* overladen with vicious carving and artificial sheen, have to answer a worse charge than that of mere extravagance. In the one case material, and in the other decoration, is utterly misapplied.

The woodcut on the preceding page illustrates a wash-hand-stand executed by Messrs. Jackson and Graham. It is of very simple construction, the only ornament introduced in it being a few easily-worked mouldings and a little inlay of coloured woods. It is intended to be made of oak, or ebonised mahogany, and fitted with a marble top.

A room intended for repose ought to contain nothing which can fatigue the eye by complexity. How many an unfortunate invalid has lain helpless on his bed, condemned to puzzle out the pattern of the hangings over his head, or stare at a wall which he feels instinctively obliged to map out into grass plots, gravel paths, and summer-houses, like an involuntary landscape gardener? Time was when a huge 'four-poster' was considered indispensable to every sleeping apartment, and night-capped gentlemen drew around their drowsy heads ponderous curtains, which bade fair to stifle them before the morning. Let us consider the gloom, the unwholesomeness, the absurdity of such a custom, viewed by our modern notions of health and comfort, and remember whatever the upholsterers tell us, that the fashion of *our* furniture, too, includes many follies at which posterity will smile.

To the four-poster succeeded the wooden canopied

bedstead, or, as it is called in the shops, the 'half-tester,' and the French bedstead, of which the head and footpiece were in shape and size alike, and over which two curtains fell, sometimes from a pole fixed at the side, and sometimes from a small circular canopy attached to the ceiling. These forms are still in use, though iron and brass are fast displacing mahogany and rosewood, as materials in their manufacture. For obvious reasons, and especially in large towns, this is a change for the better, though it is to be regretted that we lose the natural beauty of those woods, which frequently compensated for much bad design.

The design of iron bedsteads is generally very poor, especially where anything in the shape of decoration is introduced. For instance, it is usual to conceal the joint which occurs where the tie rods intersect each other with a small boss. A circular rosette would be obviously the most appropriate feature to introduce at this joint, whether in wrought or cast metal. But, instead of this, the iron-bedstead maker (*elegantiæ gratiâ*, as the grammarians say), insists on inventing a lumpy bit of ornament, which, possibly intended to represent a cluster of leaves, more closely resembles a friendly group of garden slugs, and this excrescence is repeated not only a dozen times in one bedstead, but in some thousands of the same pattern. The framework for the canopy overhead is generally far too weak for its purpose, and often vibrates with the least movement, causing infinite annoyance to invalids and nervous people. In old days the outside corners of this canopy were frequently suspended from the ceiling ; and this plan is still advisable when the supporting brackets are found to be ricketty. But if they were of stout iron and properly constructed they would need no such support.

In the decoration of iron bedsteads, and indeed all articles of domestic use executed in the same material, the paint should not be allowed to shine. Venetian red, chocolate, and sage green will perhaps be the best colours to adopt for this purpose.

Some of the ordinary modern brass bedsteads are of superior manufacture, stronger and better designed than those of iron. In selecting them, however, it will be well to choose those which are composed of simple bars and rods. I refer, of course, to those kept for general sale. At the art furniture shops, cleverly designed brass bedsteads are occasionally to be met with, but they are, as a rule, very expensive.

Many people now-a-days prefer, on sanitary grounds, to sleep, through the winter as well as the summer, in beds without hangings of any kind. It is difficult to conceive, however, that in a well-ventilated apartment, a canopy and head curtains can be at all prejudicial to health, and it is certain that they may be made to contribute not a little to the picturesqueness of a modern bed-room.

The question of their material should, of course, depend on the general aspect of the room, the nature of the carpet, wall-paper, &c. When the colour of the latter is decided in tone, white dimity curtains will by contrast have an excellent effect, particularly if the dominant colour which surrounds them is repeated in the form of braid or other trimming at their edges. But white curtains rapidly soil in London, and except in houses where they can be continually replaced, it will be better to let the bedroom paper be light, and have the curtains made of *Cretonne*, chintz, or printed cotton, which materials are now manufactured in patterns of very good design. They should never be made longer than is necessary for actual use. If they hang within two or three inches of the floor it will be quite near enough. When of greater length they trail upon the carpet and get soiled at their edges, or when drawn back they have to be looped up and pulled *over* the cord which confines them to their place. This is a most ugly and foolish fashion. Curtains, whether for a window or a bed, should be simply tied back when not in use (as in Plate XXVII.) The disposing them in heavy and artificial folds, such as one sees depicted sometimes at one corner of a theatrical drop-scene or behind the 'portrait of a gentleman' at the Royal Academy, is one out of many instances which might be quoted to illustrate the perversion of modern taste in such matters.

The canopy may be either disposed in plaits or decorated with fringe, but where plaits are used the fringe should be omitted, as it is apt to get tangled and pull the plaits out of shape. Box plaits are the best to use, and should never be less than four or five inches in width, at intervals of about eight or ten. They should be pressed down as flat as possible, and, when necessary, may be kept in shape by a stitch on either side.

Our English notions of cleanliness would scarcely permit us to tolerate any kind of coverlet for a bed which could not be periodically washed. Hence the modern counterpane, in some form or another, is likely to remain in permanent use for our beds, though it must be confessed that both in design and material it has greatly degenerated from the quality of those made

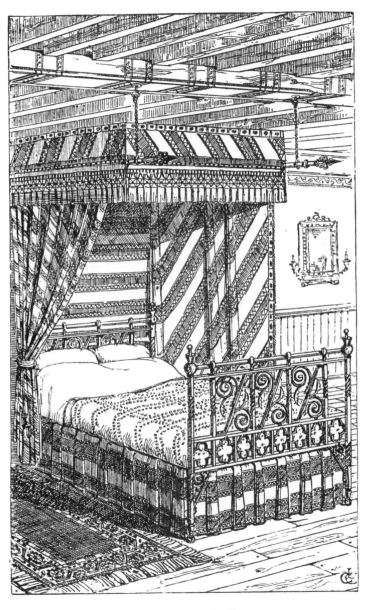

XXVII

Iron Bedstead, with Canopy,
designed by Charles L. Eastlake.

some five-and-twenty years ago. From an artistic point of view the counterpanes now manufactured for servants' bed-rooms, in which coloured thread is introduced for the knotted pattern on a grey or white ground, are very suggestive in colour; but I fear that any approach to this style of coverlet would be considered objectionable in 'best' bed-rooms.*

The striped 'Austrian' blankets which have been lately offered for sale in London shops indicate a certain tendency towards the picturesque in design, but unfortunately the colours hitherto used for them are, like most modern dyes, far too crude and violent in contrast to satisfy artistic taste.

Carpets are now so universally used to cover every portion of the floors throughout an English house, that few people find themselves comfortable without one, yet there is no doubt that the old custom of laying down a bed-side rug, and leaving the rest of the floor bare, was, especially in London houses, where dust accumulates so insidiously and rapidly, a healthier and more cleanly, as well as a more picturesque, fashion that that now in vogue.

---

* Messrs. Wanklyn, O'Hanlon and Co., of Manchester, have lately produced some counterpanes from my design at a very reasonable price.

Bed-room chairs of modern manufacture are, as a rule, of simpler, and therefore of better design, than those made for the drawing-room. Some very fair examples have of late been executed for this purpose, but perhaps the best which can be found ready-made are the rush-bottomed 'nursery chairs,' of which the woodwork is stained black, with low seats and high backs. They are still to be bought in the East of London, and traditionally retain in their general shape the spirit of an earlier and better style of work than is common in more luxurious furniture.

As a lady's taste is generally allowed to reign supreme in regard to the furniture of bed-rooms, I must protest humbly but emphatically against the practice which exists of encircling toilet-tables with a sort of muslin petticoat, generally stiffened by a crinoline of pink or blue calico. Something of the same kind may be occasionally seen twisted round the frame of the toilet-glass. They just represent a milliner's notion of the 'pretty,' and nothing more. Drapery of this kind neither is wanted nor ought to be introduced in such places. In London, especially, where dust and blacks collect whenever the bed-room window is open, it should be avoided. A toilet table with a marble top, and a few convenient little drawers, is a cleaner and infinitely preferable contrivance, and, though more costly at first, saves something in the weekly washing bill.

The above woodcut, representing a toilet table executed by Messrs. Jackson and Graham, will show

how a little alteration in the details of mouldings and
carving may give a picturesque character to such
articles of furniture without departing from the general
form which custom and convenience have prescribed.
The best and most convenient chests of drawers for
bedroom use are those which are made of solid wood
(not veneered) and which are rectangular in shape, not
bulging out in front. Even those executed in mahogany for ordinary sale might be improved by being
stained black and fitted with white metal drawer-rings
and lock escutcheons. But here again a slight modification of the conventional type will make all the
difference in the design, as may be noticed in examining the specimens exhibited at any art furniture establishment.

For practical purposes drawers are generally far too
deep. Everyone knows the inconvenience of being
obliged to delve down below innumerable strata of
clothes to find a coat or waistcoat which is wanted in
a hurry. A depth of five or six inches is quite sufficient for a single drawer of ordinary use, and by the
additional height thus gained in the whole chest,
another drawer may be added to the set. It is also
desirable that the sides of the chest (i.e. the framework
which supports the drawers) should project a little

beyond their fronts. This will be found to give a greater look of stability to the whole, and it also affords

an opportunity to introduce a little decoration in the way of mouldings or carved-work to relieve the rigid box-shaped appearance which characterises this piece of furniture as it is usually constructed.*

With a little alteration in design the modern hanging-press could be made a very picturesque, as it certainly is a most serviceable, article of domestic use. But here again the ordinary upholsterer condemns us to adopt his own notions of elegance by *rounding off* corners which in a legitimately constructive sense can only be angular—shaping panels into extravagant curves, gluing on strips of paltry and meaningless scroll-work, and surmounting the press with a heavy and uninteresting cornice. Now the cost involved by this mode of decoration and by lacquering the whole woodwork with French polish, would be sufficient to pay for a soundly-made oak or mahogany wardrobe, which by the general proportions of its form, and a few judiciously introduced mouldings, might become a really artistic feature. The following woodcut represents a wardrobe combining a hanging-press with drawers. It is executed by Messrs. Jackson and Graham, who have also a double-winged wardrobe of larger size but in the same style of workmanship. In

---

* The design represented on the preceding page is for a chest of drawers which may occasionally be used for a toilet table in a small dressing-room. It is of course not intended for ladies' use.

this instance as in many others, improved taste can only
be effected by the dictates of common sense, and it

should be always borne in mind that increase of cost,
while it may help to enrich furniture, can never invest
it with the true spirit of good design.

Chapter IX.

CROCKERY.

ROM the earliest periods of civilisation down to the present time there is, perhaps, no branch of manufacture which has undergone such vicissitudes of taste and excellence of workmanship as that of pottery. In ancient Greece, within the space of a few centuries, it not only grew from a species of rude handicraft into a refined and graceful art, but declined again so emphatically in style and quality that the purest Greek vases in Pliny's time had become of immense value, and were frequently exhumed from the tombs with the same kind of zeal which inspires a modern antiquary.

In the Middle Ages, Italy produced, under the general name of *majolica*, some of the most beautiful specimens of the ceramic art which the world has seen; but the excellence of that ware was continually varying, sometimes with the local materials at hand, sometimes with the chemical knowledge, and sometimes with the patronage of the day. In later times, the design of our own English pottery has been subject to like influences. The qualities which distinguish old Chelsea, Derby, Worcester, and Plymouth china are well known to connoisseurs. But they are qualities which, whether good or bad, are characteristic of their age, and are not likely to be reproduced in our own time.

For many years past the manufacture of Oriental ware has been steadily deteriorating, and this fact is in a great measure due to the increased facilities of our intercourse with India, and to the bad influence of modern European taste on native art. Ignorant people, who sneer at what they consider to be the artificial value set on quaint pieces of old crockery, little know what artistic merit is frequently embodied in their designs, or by what exquisite details of pattern they excel the inventions of the nineteenth century. I believe the time will come when some of those rare examples of ancient work will be worth their weight in gold, and will be sought after not so much to fill the cabinet of the antiquary or adorn the studio of the painter, but to serve as models for future imitation, when we shall have learnt that the principles of good design are not confined to mere objects of luxury, but are applicable to every sort and condition of manufacture. Does not Nature herself teach this great truth ? Many of the tender plants which we cultivate in a greenhouse must have grown wild somewhere. They may surpass the flowers of our English hedge-rows in fulness of leaf or delicacy of hue, but the humblest daisy or buttercup which springs on meadow land is as much a work of High Art, as perfect of its kind, and certainly fulfils the same eternal laws of floral growth as they obey.

It is much to be regretted that all this is lost sight of in the system of modern English design. At the china-shops especially, we shall find that almost every article of humble use or modest price is fashioned in a coarse and clumsy way—not because greater elegance of form would involve more labour—but because it is considered superfluous to aim at simple grace at all for objects which are not refined in quality of material and mode of manufacture. Now, perfection of quality and excessive accuracy in workmanship may add to the *luxe*, but never to the spirit of true art. On the contrary, there may be a sickly kind of high finish and an ignoble symmetry in design which will detract from its merit if it be good, and render it con-temptible if it be poor. I have before me at the present moment two specimens of foreign pottery—

one a preserve jar of Indian manufacture, the other an Algerine or Moorish plate. I doubt whether the most skilful craftsman in Staffordshire or at Sèvres could devise any object more thoroughly artistic in design, or better adapted for their respective purposes; and yet they are roughly-executed pieces of native ware, produced at a price doubtless not greater than that which we pay for the commonest mugs and platters at a village fair. I bought them of a London curiosity dealer for some few shillings a-piece. I suppose they could not have been made here for as many guineas.

The plate, or rather circular dish (for it is deep and capacious), is made of a coarse clay covered with an opaque glaze. In the centre, or hollow portion, is painted on a white ground, and in various colours, a very remarkable pattern. The idea seems to have been taken from a ship, for there are masts and sails, and pennants flying, and port-holes, and a patch of bluish-green below, which I suppose must be accepted as typical of water. But in such haste has the artist been to make his dish gay with colour and a pleasant flow of lines, that no one can say which is the bow and which the stern of his vessel—whether we are looking at her athwart or alongships—where the sea ends and the ship's side begins; and, finally, what relation the improbable hulk bears to the impossible rigging. The whole thing is, pictorially considered, absolute nonsense, and yet, as a bit of decorative painting, excellent. The design, such as it is, has been sketched in, evidently by hand, rapidly but with great spirit; the out-

line has been first made in brown colour, and the spaces thus marked out are filled in sometimes with flat and sometimes with accidentally gradated tints of blue, violet, green, and yellow. The picture, if we may so call it, is then enclosed in a sort of scalloppattern border, and the outside rim of the dish is

further decorated with a sort of rough-and-ready triangular patchwork of green, white, and yellow, arranged
alternately.

The Indian preserve jar is somewhat more refined
in regard both to material and style of decoration.
The ground colour here is that beautiful hue which one

might call green when opposed to blue, and blue when
opposed to green.   On this a floriated pattern is drawn
in black outline, and so profusely distributed that
scarcely a quarter of an inch square is left uncovered
by it.   There are stalks and leaves, tendrils, buds, and
flowers—none of a strictly botanical character, yet all
sufficiently suggestive of nature to be graceful.   The
stalks and leaves are of vegetable green, the tendrils

are white, the buds alternately yellow and rose pink, and the flowers of a delicate carnation gradated into light grey. All this ornament is executed in enamelled colour, slightly relieved, but unshaded and conventional in character; and on the ground thus formed are introduced at opposite sides of the circular jar four lemon-coloured discs, about three inches in diameter, decorated with Indian characters in light red, and outlined like the rest of the ornament in black. The base of the jar is bordered with yellow leaves, lapping over each other. The effect of the whole is excellent; and although, I fear, it would violate some scientific theories of chromatic harmony, one may well dispense with theories in so admirable a result.

Now, if a French or British modern porcelain painter had taken a ship or a fair flowering plant for his model, he would have gone to work in a much more knowing way. We should have seen a sloop or cutter —drawn in unexceptionable perspective—scudding with reefed topsails before the wind, or firing a salute to the port-admiral; all the tackle would have been correctly indicated; and there would have been a mountainous coast-line, or a setting sun, or a group of clouds by way of background. In like manner, the flower-painting would have been naturalistic, with shaded leaves and picturesque entanglement of stems, and, perhaps, a bunch or so of ribbon to tie them up with. And the European designer would have flattered himself on his enlightened skill, and felt inwardly grateful that he had received what is called an art-education, instead of remaining in barbaric ignorance, like the poor Bengalese or Algerine potters. But, in point of fact, his work would have been—nay, *is*—inferior to their work, and will remain so until our schools of design form a new standard of taste, and become more emphatic in their teaching.

Private energy has, however, done much towards a reform in ceramic art. The name of Wedgwood in the last century, and that of Minton in our own time, are well known as those of men who have worked with a definite purpose to that end ; and if their efforts have not resulted in a permanent revolution of public taste, we may at least be grateful to them for much of the improvement which has taken place during the last fifty years in the design of English crockery.

Excellent specimens of Minton's ware are to be found at the establishments of their London agents. Among these examples, the larger objects, such as vases, flower-dishes and figure pieces in imitation of majolica, are the most tasteful and effective in form and colour. Some of the table-china is tolerable in what may be called the *motive* of its design, but as a rule our dinner and tea services are marred by an over-neatness in the execution of their patterns, and by a tendency towards mere prettiness in the tints employed to enrich them.* Half the interest of Oriental, and indeed of all old china, depends on the artistic freedom with which it was decorated by actual handiwork ; and though in this branch of manufacture, as in many others, mechanical aid has supplanted manual labour, there can be no reason why arabesques and other surface ornament should be printed with that mathematical precision of line which represents the opposite edges of a leaf as they never are in nature—absolutely identical in contour.

The *quality* of colour applied in the decoration of modern china is generally bad. Your pinks, mauves, magentas, and other hues of the same kind, however charming they may appear in the eyes of a court-milliner, are ignoble and offensive to the taste of a real artist, and are rendered more so in our porcelain by the fact of their being laid on in perfectly flat and

---

* The thick and highly lustrous glaze which covers almost all modern crockery is much to be deplored. The worst instance of its use may be noticed in what is called ‘Irish porcelain’—a detestable ware of recent invention, which glistens like wet barley-sugar.

even tints. It has been truly said that all noble colour, whether in pictorial or decorative art, will be found *gradated*, and on this point Nature herself may be quoted as a supreme authority.

The practice of gilding china, as it is at present carried out, is a most objectionable one. It may be fairly questioned whether the application of gilding at all, looking to the nature of the material and the conditions of its manufacture, is satisfactory. But the fashion of gilding the edges of cups and plates, and *touching up*, as it were, the relieved ornament on lids and handles with streaks of gold, is a monstrous piece of vulgarity.

I have often wondered how it happens that some of the most beautiful modern dinner-services we see are so frequently spoilt by the clumsy and utterly incongruous shape of the handles with which the vegetable dishes, soup tureens, &c., are crowned. It seems, however, that, in accordance with the true spirit of modern British manufacture, the designer of the mould in which these vessels are shaped knows nothing of the surface pattern which they are subsequently to receive. The consequence is that, as the mould represents an expensive item in the manufacture, and has often, when once executed, to serve for a dozen different patterns, the pattern designer has to take the *shape* of his dishes just as he finds it, however ugly it may be. Surely grace of form is too important an element of beauty to be thus neglected! If it is desirable for economy's sake that one mould should suffice for many surface patterns, then it is all the more necessary that that form should be in every respect a graceful one. A simple ring or round knob would be an infinitely better handle for dish-covers, &c., than the twisted stalks, gilt acorns, sea-shells, and other silly inventions which we find so constantly repeated on them, and which, while they are contemptible in a poor design, are destructive to the effect of a good one.

There has been a great improvement of late years in the design of ordinary water-jugs. I bought a very good one for four shillings some time ago in the Strand, under the trade name of 'antique.' It is introduced in the sketch of bed-room drawers, p. 215. The lower portion was bulbous; the neck straight but not narrow, and covered with a metal top ; the handle long and of a simple loop form. The material was a cream-coloured stone ware. Round the bowl and neck were scarlet bands enriched with round and diamond-shaped lozenges placed alternately. These lozenges contained quatrefoil panels of enamelled colour (dark blue and rose-pink). My jug was about eight inches high, but I believe the same pattern might have been had in various sizes. I say ' might *have been* had,' for I fear a good design rarely keeps its place in the market. So long as it is new it sells well enough, but next season it is thrust aside to make room for some fresh novelty. All that the British public seems to care for is to get the ' last thing out': taste is a secondary consideration. No doubt some of my readers may have noticed in the shop-windows a little flower-vase of ' biscuit,' or Parian ware, in the shape of a human hand modelled, *au naturel*, holding a narrow cup. A more commonplace and silly notion of a vase can scarcely be imagined, and yet so delighted were the public with this new conceit that it sold everywhere by hundreds. In one establishment alone twelve men were constantly employed in producing relays of this article. I suppose by this time everybody has discovered that his neighbour has bought it, and all pronounce it commonplace.

The manufacture of modern pottery in England includes no better example of good design applied to cheap and useful objects than the red ' delf' ware, originally produced, I believe, by Wedgwood, but now adopted by most of the leading firms for a variety of articles to which this material is especially suited. It is to be had in all shades of colour, from a pale ochreous hue to a deep Indian red. Almost all these tints are very beautiful in themselves, but their effect is sometimes marred by the use of enamelled colour applied in too violent a contrast. The unglazed ware is used for water-bottles, butter-coolers, &c., its porous nature being admirably adapted for such purposes. It is, however, much to be regretted that after a period of about twelve months these vessels begin to fail in their object. The water exudes only from their lower surface, and they seem to be no longer porous elsewhere. I have tried to ascertain the cause of this, and am told that the clay, from constant exposure to the air and touch, becomes hardened or clogged with dust. It is said that placing them in a hot oven, and washing them with fine sand, will restore their porous quality; but I am inclined to think that the imperfection is gradually produced by the water itself, which probably leaves a deposit of lime in passing through to the surface. They are, however, sufficiently cheap to be replaced from time to time in most households, and are certainly very elegant and picturesque specimens of industrial art. The most ordinary form of delf water-bottle is bulbous at its lower end, with a narrow neck, the upper part of which, being most exposed to the touch, is very properly glazed. Both the neck and the body of the jug are frequently decorated with enamelled colour arranged in geometrical patterns of a Greek or mediæval character. Some of the water-bottles take the form of small antique vases, and these are, for the

most part, made of plain clay. Very beautiful examples of this class, in 'orange porous' delf, may now be bought for a few shillings a-piece. The same material is frequently used for tea-pots, hot water-jugs, &c., the ware, either red or stone colour, being in these cases covered internally with a glaze. The tea-service illustrated on this page, and manufactured by Messrs. Copeland, of Bond Street, is a fair example of this class. A

few years ago some mustard-pots and salt-cellars of excellent design were produced in this material. They
were generally decorated with bands of enamelled
colour, and silver mounted. Infinitely more tasteful
than the ordinary class of articles which deck the
dinner-table, they were offered for sale at a price within
reach of the most economical household (I believe
about 5*s.* 6*d.* the pair). In spite of these recommenda-
tions, they met with very few purchasers, and though
still kept in stock at certain shops, they are rarely asked
for. In this and a hundred other instances it is the
public taste which is at fault, and manufacturers can
hardly be blamed for discontinuing to bring out works
of sound art which are *caviare* to the multitude.

Even when a good design does by any chance get
into vogue, it is only in demand for a limited time, and
makes way for the last novelty which has tickled the
fancy of a fashionable few. Not long ago there was a
run upon toilet services of white stone ware, decorated
with a simple monochrome border—viz., either the
guilloche (wave) pattern, or some variation of the
Greek *fret* (familiarly known as the 'key'). Now
either of these patterns is excellent of its kind, and
well adapted to the purpose. But they were gradually displaced by a new conceit. Some designer,

with more ingenuity than good taste, hit upon the notion that pink and mauve ribbons, twisted backwards and forwards in a series of symmetrical loops, would form a fitting ornament for the neck of an ewer, and the edge of a washing basin. The notion was an absurd one, but it became popular, and the probability is that not one housewife out of ten cared to consider what possible connection there could be between cap-ribbons and a bed-room jug.* Indeed, there is no branch of art-manufacture exposed to greater dangers, in point of taste, than that of ceramic design. Nor is it by any means easy to lay down specific rules for the guidance of even a general taste which is inexperienced in this department of art. The tendency of the uneducated eye is, in most cases, to admire the smart and showy but effeminate hues of the day rather than the subtle and refined combinations of colour which distinguish ancient pottery and porcelain. Extravagance of form is preferred to a sober grace of contour, and neatness of execution to the spirit of artistic design. The 'pretty,' in short, is too frequently held in higher estimation than the beautiful, and nothing but ex-

---

* The forms of swans and bulrushes, sea-weed and ivy, have since been pressed into this special service, whether by the caprice of the manufacturer or the bad taste of the public, I will not venture to say. In either case the result is melancholy to contemplate.

perience, based on a frequent inspection of good examples, with a general knowledge of, and reverence for, the principles of sound art, will teach people to value the importance of this distinction.

To a reasoning mind, however, which recognises the necessity of discriminating between pictorial and decorative art, it will be obvious that if their respective conditions are ever to be maintained inviolate, they must be so in this particular field. The representation of perspective, of aërial effect, and of chiaroscuro would be impossible on surfaces which, independently of the consideration of texture, are liable to every variety of contour. The Greeks understood this principle so well that they contented themselves, as we find on all antique vessels, with representing the human figure and other objects on one flat colour, red (and sometimes white) on a black ground, or *vice versâ*. The folds of drapery, the action of limbs, &c., were expressed by lines. There was no shading, or pictorial effect. The design was simply decorative, and depended for its beauty on exquisite drawing, correct symmetry of general form, and refinement of execution. The principles of design in Greek pottery have been from time to time revived and applied to modern manufacture with more or less success, but the great expense attending the reproduction of antique designs has

XXVIII

Greek Toilet Ware,

manufactured by Messrs. Copeland.

hitherto formed the chief obstacle to such revivals. A few leading firms have, however, lately endeavoured to overcome this difficulty; and it is satisfactory to know that at their establishments many articles of household use, as, for instance, bed-room jugs and basins, toilet-ware, &c., can now be procured in this class of ware at a cost which does not exceed the average price of such articles—at least when they are the best of their kind.

The ewers retain the form prevalent for ordinary use, which is hardly worthy of their surface decoration, but the toilet-ware, of which a few specimens are given in Plate XXVIII, is also excellent in general form, and reflects great credit on its manufacturers, in regard both to material and workmanship. If we compare such objects as these with the showy but commonplace crockery which we find decorated with ribbons and bunches of flowers, it is impossible to avoid the conclusion that strictly pictorial representations of nature are quite unsuitable to the true conditions of design in ceramic art; and we find this principle realised not only in the Classic age, but in all the best periods of manufacture which have succeeded it. The early Italian majolica, though differing widely in sentiment of design and quality of material from antique pottery, embodies no realisms in its ornament. Portraits (so-called) are indeed introduced in the 'marriage-plates' of that period, but they are little more than conventional representations; and I question whether they would ever have been recognised without the addition of a label or other device on which the name of the fair bride 'Elena diva,' or 'Bella Marta,' was usually inscribed.

To this early period of Italian majolica (about the first half of the sixteenth century) I would especially draw attention, as realising in its manufacture some of the highest artistic qualities which can be associated in ceramic manufacture—viz., beauty and vigour of form, thorough harmony of colour, and propriety of ornament. Some exquisite specimens may be seen at the Kensington Museum, and cannot be too carefully examined by those who desire a standard of excellence in the art which is there so ably illustrated.*

The ancient wares of Gubbio, of Urbino, and Faenza, are especially famous. From the name of the latter

---

* Mr. W. S. Coleman, in his figure-subject designs for modern ware, manufactured by Messrs. Minton & Co. at their art-pottery works, has realised much of the true spirit of old majolica. Those specimens which are painted by the artist's own hand are of course expensive; but dinner services and articles of ordinary household use have been executed under his superintendence, at a more moderate price, for general sale.

place the French word *faïence* is derived, but was subsequently applied to a very different species of manufacture. The term *Raphaelesque* is sometimes given
indiscriminately to the majolica of Raphael's own time
and to that which was produced years after his death,
but which was painted in imitation of his pictorial
works. However interesting the latter may be by
reason of its connection with the inventions of so great
an artist, it can hardly be recommended as a model
for modern imitation. The colour was generally excellent, the drawing bold and masterlike; the traditional shapes of the majolica vessels were in most
cases preserved, and thus lent an additional charm to
the effect   But such surface-decoration is, after all, an
incomplete picture, and must appear to anyone acquainted with the original works in the light of a rude
and clumsy copy.

Some of the purest majolica of Raphael's time is
enriched with the delicate and elegant arabesque, in
which we trace the spirit of that decorative ornament
which graces the Loggie of the Vatican. Even the
rudest specimens of this ware are admirable in their
scheme of colour and in motive of ornament. The
ground is generally white—not the crude white of
modern porcelain, but a mellow creamy hue well adapted

to relieve the colours laid over it; these are generally raw sienna and Indian yellows, scored with lines of reddish brown; of blues there are several shades, light indigo being most chiefly, and *turquoise* most sparingly used: light copper green and Indian red complete the list of tints. The ornament is swiftly but spiritedly drawn in a series of fantastically-conceived figures, which terminate in light tendril-shaped lines and buds of colour. Where the human figure is introduced, it is sketched roughly, but with evident knowledge. The general form of dishes, plates, salt-cellars, and other specimens of this ware is well accentuated, but not rigidly symmetrical in outline. There is no *compass* accuracy about them; nor is the material of which they are composed uniformly faultless. In some parts the glaze may be a little thinner than in others, and here and there we may perchance light upon an air-hole. The colour on the right side of a platter may be less forcible than it is on the left. But all these are defects of little moment in the eyes of an artist who recognises the dexterity and cunning of the hands that moulded the clay and decorated its surface.* At present the

---

* Among the French specimens of ceramic art in the International Exhibition of 1872 the *faïence* of T. Deck, and the *Manufacture de Gien*, from Loiret, by Geoffroy & Cie, may be mentioned as admirable in design and workmanship. Most of them are hand-painted, but a few small

price of artistic labour obliges us to rely upon machine-printing for the decoration of our cheaper crockery, and therefore the treatment of the original design becomes of the highest importance. In the manufacture of stone ware the Belgians have set us a good example by their reproduction of old *Grès-de-Flandres* moulded from good old models and often excellent in colour. It is one of the most satisfactory instances which I know of improved taste in industrial art, and might with advantage be imitated in this country, where we possess great executive skill with but little conceptional taste.* In designing and executing the cheaper kinds of hard porcelain, the French far surpass us. Some very good toilet-services, bed-room candlesticks, and chimney-piece match-boxes were imported some years ago, and I believe are still brought from France, although they are sometimes stamped with British

examples, either partially or wholly printed, show how successfully mechanical aid may be applied in the reproduction of majolica and old Rouen ware. A depôt for the Gien pottery has recently been opened by M. Oppenheim, at 21 Park Side, Albert Gate.

* The grey and buff stone-ware recently produced by Doulton & Co. of Lambeth, affords evidence of improved taste in British pottery. The quality of the ware (hitherto chiefly employed for beer jugs and such small articles) is excellent, and some of the designs are good in general form, though capable of much improvement in the style of surface decoration. To secure this, the manufacturers could hardly do better than copy the beautiful specimens of old *Grès-de-Flandres* which may be procured at a trifling cost from some of our curiosity dealers.

trade-marks. These articles are made of a thin white porcelain, the surface of which is decorated with figures, &c., printed in a fine brown outline, and then filled in by hand (before the second firing) with flat colour. These figure-groups are generally of a quasi-classical character: dancing nymphs, gladiatorial fights and chariot races, are the favourite subjects. Sometimes a single head appears as a medallion on the side of a little vase. The drawing is usually very fair in execution. There is no shading, the folds of drapery, &c., being expressed by outline only. The colours are well selected, and, considering the very low price at which it is offered for sale, this toilet ware is a great improvement on anything of the kind which has been produced for ordinary sale during the last twenty years. It appears to be supplied in London at the toy and fancy warehouses rather than by regular dealers in china. Some specimens bear the letters 'B. Co.' on a sort of trade mark. This china is probably manufactured at Limoges, where many such articles are produced in porcelain at a price with which our manufacturers cannot hope to compete. But in the manufacture of earthenware, regarding both cheapness and quality, England still stands unrivalled.

Chapter X.

TABLE GLASS.

EXT to a good display of china on the table or sideboard, there is nothing which lends greater grace to the appointments of a dining-room than delicate and well-designed glass. North of the Tweed, it is not unusual to regard 'crystal' as the all-important feature of domestic feasts; and certainly most London housewives who can afford the luxury are as careful of the appearance of their decanters and wine-glasses as the glittering plate which lies beside them. The same national peculiarity which makes us fastidious to secure spotless purity in our table-linen and a mirror-like smoothness for our French-polished wood, leads us also to require that every article of glass which we use shall be absolutely free from flaws or blemishes of every kind. Now it is easy to see that a demand for this sort of perfection, although it may tend to make admirable housemaids and laundresses, does not do much to promote the interests of art. I suppose there are no houses in the world kept so scrupulously clean and neat internally as a well-appointed English house; no carriages so luxurious and well finished in manufacture as ours; no boots so well blacked as British boots—and yet our dwellings are uninteresting, our best equipages unpicturesque, and our dress is as ugly as that of the rest of Christendom.

Much the same might have been said up to within the last few years, and, indeed, may to a great extent still be said, of our ordinary table glass. Most householders can recollect a time when the great test of excellence in such articles depended on the question whether they were 'cut' or not. If they were cut at all they were considered good; if they were cut elaborately they were 'elegant;' if they were only blown they were worthless. It did so happen that at that time, bad as the cut glass was, the blown glass was rather worse; but this may be chiefly attributed to the fact that the latter was blown into a mould, which was frequently shaped so as to imitate the effect of cutting. Our manufacturers seem quite to have forgotten that the most beautiful table glass which has ever been produced—viz., that of Venice in the fifteenth century —was not 'cut,' in the modern sense of the word, at all.

Those of my readers who have seen specimens of this exquisite and ancient art in public or private museums must be quite aware how much it differs from the heavy and inelegant vessels from which our grandfathers drank their port and sherry.

The author of 'Modern Painters,' in one of those long but interesting digressions with which his volumes abound, once took occasion, while commenting on the degraded state of modern art-manufacture, to ridicule the national pride with which we English are accustomed to regard the characteristics of our modern table glass. 'We ought rather,' adds Mr. Ruskin, 'to be ashamed of it.'

This opinion, startling as it may sound in the ears of those who are accustomed to back British goods generally against the world, is nevertheless founded on principles of science as well as of art. The process of manufacture which every raw material undergoes before it is converted into objects of practical utility, and, consequently, the form which such objects finally assume, ought to depend chiefly, if not entirely, on the natural properties of the material itself. Whenever this principle is lost sight of, the result appears either in the light of a technical defect or an æsthetic error. For instance, we know that, inasmuch as the strength of iron depends on the density and tenacity of its fibre, the repeated processes of heating and hammering must be the best means of securing that strength ; whereas cast-iron, which takes its artificial form while in a state of fusion, though cheaper in its cost of production, is much weaker than that which is wrought. Again, as a matter of taste, wrought-iron ornament, such as that, for example, which decorates the pump of Quentin Matsys at Antwerp, is infinitely more artistic than the clumsy cast-iron railings which too often surround our public buildings. In one case the design has been suggested by the natural capabilities of the material ; in the other the nature of the material has been perverted for the sake of a specious and inappropriate method of treatment.

The same distinction, and with a like reason, may be drawn between ancient and modern table glass. The former was generally blown, the natural ductility of the material being such that while in a state of partial fusion it could be stamped, twisted, and fashioned into shapes which varied with the individual taste and skill of the workman. The consequence was that in Venice, during the fifteenth and two following centuries, this branch of art-industry rose to a pitch of excellence which obtained for it a world-wide reputation. It would

be impossible to enumerate here all the peculiar varieties
of design included in this ingenious and beautiful art.
Under the general head of 'filagree' glass, the combinations of form and colour (including that of the
well-known *latticinio*) were countless. Then there
were the *millefiori*, in which slices of rod-glass appeared embedded in a colourless or differently-coloured
ground of the same material ; the *schmelze*, or mock
agate ; the *avventurino*, with its rich golden lustre
which has been basely imitated in modern toilet-trinkets ;
the 'crackle' and 'opal' glass in which light is refracted
with exquisite effect, and many other kinds which were
further enriched by the distinct processes of enamelling
and engraving. Up to this time the early traditions
of the art had been preserved, or perhaps revived
from the time of the Romans, when glass was blown
in moulds, stamped, turned on a wheel and engraved,
rudely enough sometimes, but often with great artistic
care. The celebrated Portland vase, for instance, was
probably made of two layers of glass, of which the
upper surface was cut away in cameo-fashion, to
form a background for the bas-relief with which it is
decorated. But work of so laborious and costly a
character as this must, of course, be regarded as ex-
ceptional. The ordinary table glass made in Venice

and exported to every country in Europe during the early part of the ' Renaissance,' was for the most part blown only, and depended for its form on the taste and manipulation of artisans, whose fancy was as fertile as their fingers were apt, and who required no school of design to teach them the shape of a flask or beaker.

Unfortunately for the interests of Art, a taste grew up in the eighteenth century for the imitation of crystal. Now, without entering into scientific details, it is sufficient to remember that glass is formed by the combination of silica (sand or flint) with an alkali, or with oxide of lead. These, on the application of heat, fuse into colourless transparent liquids, and finally cool into hard brittle solids, having an amorphous or non-crystalline character. It is true that under rare conditions, similar to those which result, for instance, in the production of what is called Réaumur's porcelain, the formation of crystals may be determined by the application of heat lower than that necessary to effect the perfect fusion of the glass. But then that material, which is opaque in substance, has become actually devitrified, and can hardly be called glass at all. Any attempt, therefore, to give ordinary glass, such as is manufactured for drinking vessels, &c., the appearance of cut crystal, is to treat it in a manner foreign to its real nature. Our manufacturers not only aimed at this, but, by the employment of *minium* (red lead) in large quantities, they endeavoured to invest their table glass with a peculiar brightness which it is almost impossible to attain without that ingredient. In this way, however, they lost two important qualities of the old material, viz., lightness and ductility. It cooled during manufacture much more rapidly than before, leaving little or no time for that delicate hand-work which we recognise in the graceful forms and fantastic ornament of Venetian glass; but these defects have until lately been almost regarded in the light of advantages.

In the manufacture of table glass, some fifty years ago, great angularity of form, lumpy ornament, deep incisions, and solidity of material were the chief characteristics of its design. Now all these are directly opposed to the natural properties of glass, which, in a state of fusion, is capable of being blown and twisted into the most light and elegant forms, fragile certainly in appearance, but capable of lasting for ages if handled with ordinary care. Old Venetian glass was of this kind; and, elaborately decorated as many of its examples are, the lightness of their weight is extraordinary. Combined with this lightness we find a peculiar elasticity of material which renders the glass hardly less brittle on the whole than the more solid-looking examples of our own time.

Now it is well to bear in mind what constitutes the material beauty of glass. If it is to be perfectly colourless and clear as water, but heavy withal, then modern English glass is the best that has been produced. But to the eye of an artist the delicate gradations of natural colour, the slight imperfections and streakiness of old glass, render it infinitely more attractive than a purity of texture which has nothing but its clearness to recommend it, and which can only be acquired by a sacrifice of more precious qualities. For the simple transmission of light through the best piece of flint glass that could be manufactured is of small value compared with the mellow and often jewel-like effect produced in the design of a Venetian beaker. In addition to this it must be remembered that table glass, to be made spotless in substance, must also be made heavy. It is the red lead employed in its manufacture which gives our glass its *weight* as well as its spotless lustre. Under these conditions of material, our manufacturers had recourse to moulding, pressing, cutting, and engraving—modes of decoration which, as they were once practised, reduced the workman to a mere machine, and left him to think of nothing but making his tumblers accurately round and his goblets perfectly symmetrical.

One of the conditions of æsthetic taste seems to be that in civilised life it shall revolve in cycles; and whether or not we may attribute the change to a certain impetus which our art manufacturers received through the Great Exhibition of 1851, it is certain that after that date a great modification took place in the design of English table glass. People began to discover that the round bulbous form of decanter was a more pleasant object to look at than the rigid outline of a pseudo-crystal pint-pot carved and chopped about into unmeaning grooves and planes. The reversed and truncated cone, which served our grandfathers as a model for wine-glasses, gradually disappeared before the lily and crocus-shaped bowls, from which we now sip our sherry and Bordeaux. Champagne had formerly been drunk from tall and narrow glasses, which required to be tossed aloft before they could be emptied. It is now a broad and shallow *tazza* which sparkles with the vintage of Epernay. For some years past the forms of our goblets and water-bottles have been gradually improving; many artistic varieties of the material have appeared, and the style of decoration employed, especially with engraved glass, is very superior to what it used to be. Some English manufacturers have even endeavoured to reproduce the most familiar types of old Venetian glass. But these imitations have hitherto been carried out in the letter rather than in the spirit of ancient work. There has been a too evident striving after perfect accuracy of form, and that ignoble neatness of execution which is fatal to the vigour of good design. If the workman is directing his energies to make a round dish mathematically correct in outline, or the opposite profiles of a jug match each other with absolute precision, he cannot be expected to work with the free hand of an artist. So our table glass was very bright, very accurately shaped, often very nicely engraved; but, on the other hand, very heavy, seldom otherwise than formal in contour, and generally unpicturesque.

In short, we have gradually given up the vigour of design, gradation of tone, brilliance of colour, as well as the lightness and elasticity of old glass, simply for the sake of getting two sides of a decanter exactly alike, and being able to see each other clearly through the centre!

In the days of the Venetian Republic, its glass was exported to every country in Europe. Its manufacturers were artists who vied with each other in the beauty of form and the fertility of invention which their designs expressed. Not many years ago this national art had degenerated into a trade which produced little more than glass beads and apothecaries' bottles. It has, however, been revived through the exertions of Dr. Salviati, himself a Venetian, but whose name is well known in this country in connection with the enamel mosaics which are now extensively used for architectural decoration. He succeeded in directing towards a worthy object the intelligence and ability of the Venetian artisans and the glass manufacturers of Murano. Many of these men were struggling in a state of poverty, for the work on which they had for many years past been employed was of the humblest description, and for this work they received the humblest wages.

The demand of the last two generations for the produce of their ancient handicraft had been so unimportant that these honest folks were reduced to earn a livelihood by plying the meanest and worse-paid branches of their trade. One of them, an ingenious native artisan, first suggested the possibility of reproducing the almost forgotten manufacture of enamel mosaics. Aided by this man's practical experience, Dr. Salviati, who himself possessed the zeal and taste of an able connoisseur, undertook a series of experiments, which resulted in the establishment of his well-known factory at Venice.

The mosaic decorations of St. Paul's, of the Wolsey Chapel at Windsor, as well as those executed for the Albert Memorial and for the altar-piece at Westminster Abbey, have since proved that the revival of so venerable and splendid an art is well appreciated in this country. But Dr. Salviati has done more for Venice. Encouraged by the advice of some English artist friends, he re-established there a manufactory of table glass, which, in quality of material, excellence of design, and spirit of workmanship, soon promised to rival anything of the kind which had been produced. Indeed, there seems little reason why it should fall short of former excellence. In England, the great difficulty of bringing about such a revival would probably be the want of skill in the art-workman. But at Murano these poor glass-blowers appear to inherit as a kind of birth-right the technical skill in a trade which made their forefathers famous.

Better wages, a more interesting occupation than they formerly enjoyed, and, perhaps, a feeling of national pride which the independence of Italy awakened, combined to encourage their efforts. Dr. Salviati did his best to procure good designs and old examples for the men to copy. A large depôt for the

XXIX.

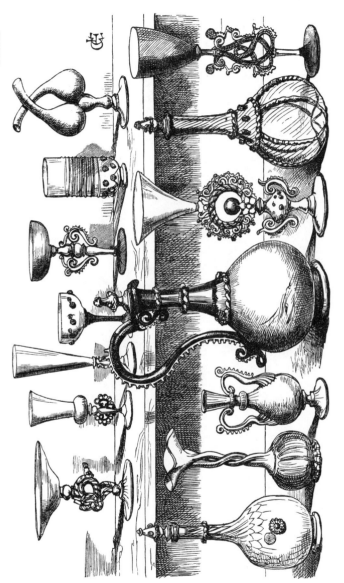

Specimens of Modern Venetian Table Glass,

manufactured by Salviati & Co.

table glass, under the management of an English company, aided by the zealous exertions and valuable advice of Mr. A. H. Layard, was opened in St. James's Street, and rapidly became popular with English customers. Here may be seen, in rich variety of form and colour, water-bottles, claret jugs, tumblers, wine and liqueur glasses, salt-cellars, preserve jars, flower-stands, tazze, vases, &c., &c., many of them very beautiful in design, and all possessing qualities of material which we seek in vain among our native ware. They have not, indeed, the cold accuracy of form and spotless sheen of an ordinary dessert service, but they are far more picturesque in appearance, wonderfully light in weight, and cheap enough to bear competition with any table glass which has pretensions to artistic merit. Some of the goblets are highly decorated below the bowl with bosses of coloured glass, conventionally-shaped flowers, and that peculiar kind of pinched-up ornament to which the Italians give the technical name *morise*. The term *ritorto* is applied to a delicately-striped glass, which is frequently made into lily-shaped bowls and dishes.

Another very beautiful kind of ware is produced by joining two thin films of glass in such a manner as to leave air-bubbles distributed in a sort of diapered pattern over its surface　This is called 'bubble filagree,' and is much prized on account of the delicacy required in its manufacture.

The old Dutch type of water-bottle, with its round capacious bowl of thin glass, strengthened at intervals with little twisted ribs of the same material, was manufactured in ancient Venice also, and frequently decorated with colour. It is now produced at the price of a common wine decanter. In like manner the sturdy green hock glasses which we once imported from Holland have been imitated and improved on by Salviati; for whereas their broad-ribbed stems were not unfrequently cast or blown into a mould, those exported from Venice have stems composed of an actual cord of glass wound spirally round, and so spreading outwards to form a foot. When *avventurino* decoration is introduced in this type of stem its appearance is very beautiful. The principal colours used are bottle-green, *turchino*, ruby, amber, olive, and *acquamarina*—a very pretty sea-blue tint, which is peculiarly characteristic of this glass. Some of the smaller tumblers are quite plain, with a delicate edging of colour round the brim. The beakers, which hold a half-pint or more, are sometimes laced round with the thinnest possible thread of coloured glass, and then, in order to give the hand a firmer grasp, the lower end of the tumbler is enriched with bosses of the same hue. I must not omit to mention the *opal* glass, which transmits a rich and lovely iridescent light, exactly like the precious stone from which it is named.*

Of course the smooth perfections and stereotyped neatness of ordinary English goods are neither aimed at nor found in this ware. But if fair colour, free grace of form, and artistic quality of material, constitute excellence in such manufacture, this is the best modern table glass which has been produced.

Technical enigmas in connection with colour and the new conditions of form had to be solved, and even the most experienced workmen required some little time before their heads and hands became accustomed to the novel character and the delicacy of the work before them. At first, as might have been expected, the specimens forwarded to England were somewhat crude in conception and a little clumsy in form. But as fresh consignments arrived, a marked improvement

---

* It is to be trusted that the characteristic charms of this glass will not suffer by connection with the British market. I regret to find that there is a demand for those specimens which include the greatest variety of colour. I have seen some goblets, for instance, in which the bowl, the stem, and the foot are all of different hues. This is a great mistake. The best examples are those in which the main body of the glass is plain, and relieved by a single colour in the ornamental portions.

was noticeable, and by degrees the Venetian glass of the nineteenth century approached in vigour of design and in the spirit of its execution, those beautiful examples which, after a lapse of nearly three centuries, still command our admiration. In this country the lovers of art-manufacture have reason to be well satisfied with the result, and, indeed, there is only one class of persons whom it is likely to displease. For many years past the examples of old Venetian glass which came to the market through public auction, or which still lingered on the shelves of old curiosity shops, have fetched a very high price; nor can we wonder at this when we remember that such fragile objects are liable to injury and breakage whenever they change hands, and that every year must diminish their number. In addition to this fact, there was, until lately, no prospect of the manufacture being revived, and that naturally enhanced their worth. But now, when almost every characteristic of the old work can be reproduced with a fidelity which surprises even the experienced connoisseur, and at about a tenth part of what it used to cost in price, the commercial value of the original ware must to some extent depreciate.

It is not too much to say for this modest but interesting effort at reform in the manufacture of table glass, that it marks an important era in the history of industrial art. In no other direction that can be named — neither in the design of cabinet-work, ceramic ware, or jewellery—have we moderns realised so nearly the tastes and excellences of a by-gone age ; and it will be a curious coincidence if, after years of humiliation and bondage, Venice should be enabled to revive one of the sources of her ancient wealth in the same epoch which has restored her to political and national freedom.

Chapter XI.

DRESS AND JEWELLERY.

AMONG the various influences to which we may attribute the decline of artistic taste and of art-manufacture during the present century, the ugliness of modern dress stands pre-eminently forward. On the painter and sculptor its effect is lamentable, compelling them, as it necessarily does, either totally to forego all representation of the age in which they live—a state of things which has never existed and could never exist in any healthy condition of art—or to undertake a difficult and thankless task, the result of which if well executed is barely interesting, and if indifferently executed is ludicrous.

The subject, although rarely considered in its æsthetic relations, has met with some degree of popular attention, and indeed may be described as one of those questions of social reform which are, from time to time, brought before the public, discussed with more or less ability, and having afforded ample scope for ingenious suggestions, are again allowed to drop into oblivion. It is the fate of our national costume—or rather of European costume (for it contains but little element of nationality)—to be treated in this manner. Male attire in this country is not only unbecoming, but frequently inconvenient to the wearer, and in some respects unhealthy.

It is, however, much more easy to censure the follies of modern dress than to propose a remedy for them, or even to assign a cause for their existence. Take, for example, the recently abandoned but once favourite article of ladies' attire—crinoline. Under the names of hoop and farthingale, it was twice in vogue in this country before it was revived for a third time in 1857. We have abundant proof that it was both ridiculed and seriously condemned by our ancestors. Yet neither satire nor sermons seem to have affected its use. All that we know is the fact that women wore it as long as it pleased them, and left it off when it ceased to do so. But the old hoop, it will be urged, seemed appropriate to the custom which accompanied it; it went well with patches, high-heeled shoes, and powdered hair. Besides, it was a more honest and less complicated affair than the modern one, and, not requiring so much stuff to cover it, involved less danger to be apprehended from fire.   But is it probable that these reasons, or any similar reasons, ensured a popularity for the hoop or farthingale which the crinoline could not command ?   Is it not a fact that, in spite of many petty inconveniences which it occasioned—in spite of its being utterly unsuitable to the rest of a lady's toilette —in spite of the charges of indelicacy and extravagance which have been so frequently brought against it—in spite of the terrible and untimely deaths which ensued from its use, this wretched invention continued in full favour with women for a full decade of years in the nineteenth century ?

Take another instance—the modern gentleman's hat, of which the beaver prototype was introduced here about the time of the French Revolution.   Could anything more ugly, more incommodious, more unhealthy, more generally objectionable, be devised as a covering for the head ?   Yet, so far from its use being discontinued, as was thought probable during the year of the first Great Exhibition, no part of a man's dress appears to be further removed from all chance of improvement than this.   No one who values his position in society —no one who cares for the public recognition of his friends—would venture to wear any substitute for it in the streets of London.   Men go on enduring this evil with aching brows—just as women have endured and will again endure similar martyrdom—simply for the sake of appearances, and because, as civilised life is now constituted, singularity of dress would be considered, in most cases, a vulgar affectation.

Hopeless as reform seems to be, in certain details of modern costume, it is satisfactory to think that some slight improvements in dress have been made during the latter half of the present century. If the Exhibition of 1851 had not the effect of exterminating the 'chimney-pot,' it brought over thousands of foreigners who had long eschewed the use of the razor. Englishmen began to ask themselves whether the prejudice against beards, which had existed in the days of the 'great unwashed'—our forefathers—should be allowed to extend to our own time, when every gentleman takes his morning bath. Was it not absurd that we should continue day by day, with no little pains and inconvenience, to rasp our faces for the purpose of removing an appendage which Nature had given us for use if not for ornament? The 'beard movement' rapidly became popular—the newspapers took up the cause, and said what they could in its favour. In the course of a few years, a clean-shaved man became the exception in a crowd. Thenceforth the hideous and uncomfortable *Vater-mörder*—the stand-up collars, which had for more than a quarter of a century prevented us from freely turning our head to the right or left, were banished from young England's wardrobe. Even the thick silk handkerchief, which succeeded to the stock, gave place at last to that light and comfortable tie or scarf which is now almost universally used with a turn-down collar.

A few recent changes in men's dress may be noted, which, without being what might be desirable in an artistic sense, are at least calculated to promote convenience. Wellington boots were, after all, only a modification of the old ' Hessian ' type, which, however convenient when pantaloons were worn, became unnecessary under the folds of the modern trouser. Accordingly the ankle-boot was adopted. At first it was fastened with buttons, and this led to the invention of the button-hook—an article which was perpetually being mislaid, and which generally tore out more buttons than it helped to fasten. But the later manufacture of ' Balmorals ' for country wear, and the ' side spring ' for ordinary use, left nothing to be desired in this respect.

Some of us recollect the old coat-collar which used to rise from the shoulders of the wearer in a padded roll until it touched the back of his head. That ungainly feature has long since resumed its proper place and proportions. The waistcoat now terminates not as formerly across the widest part of the chest, but at the waist. Even sleeves and trousers, the most uncompromising details of a man's attire, have of late been allowed to partake in general outline of the shape of the limbs which they enclose. The morning coat, though not, perhaps, as picturesque as it was a hundred years ago, is infinitely better than that which was in vogue in the early part of this century.

Still there is great room for improvement. We want a style of dress which shall be at once picturesque and comfortable. It must be fitted for the ordinary vocations of life. It must be of a material which will not get spotted or spoil in a shower. It must be of a kind which either a tall or a short man may wear without making him look conspicuous. The knickerbocker suit, for example, fulfils all these conditions admirably, and has been adopted for ordinary wear in many country gentlemen's houses. With some slight alterations in point of material, &c., it might be used very well in towns, and those who have had to walk in trousers through London mud would soon learn to appreciate the change.

Above all, our evening dress needs radical reform. How it happens that black cloth has come to be associated with occasions of public and private festivity in common with occasions of public and private mourning is a riddle which we must leave posterity to solve. But it is certain that in the existing state of society, Englishmen wear the same dress at an evening party and at a funeral. Nor is this all, for many a host who entertains his friends at dinner has a butler behind his chair who is dressed precisely like himself. To add to this confusion, the clergyman who rises to say grace might, until recently, have been mistaken for either. A few years ago it was whispered that a certain Royal personage of our own time contemplated the suggestion of a complete change in evening dress. It is only through the agency of such an example that we could ever hope to escape from the conventional ugliness of a modern tail-coat; and looking at the subject from a common-sense, as well as an artistic point of view, we must admit that attention might be turned to this matter with great benefit to the public.

With regard to ladies' costume in England at the present time, undeniably though it has improved within the last five and twenty years, all criticism on the subject is impossible, for the simple reason that the rapid changes of fashion make it useless to approve or condemn details of form and colour in dress which may be modified or actually banished from the wardrobe while these pages are being printed. There is, however, one branch of art-manufacture which, although closely associated with women's attire, is not subject to such constant variation in design, and on which I shall venture to offer a few remarks.

The word 'jewellery,' in its generally accepted and modern sense, is understood to mean ornaments worn for personal adornment only; but there was a time when gems and precious stones were employed in the decoration of almost all articles which, on account of their refined use, artistic workmanship, or sacred value, seemed worthy of such luxurious enrichment. There can be no doubt that our forefathers, even at a time when the habits of social life were rude and simple, delighted in the appearance and possession of such articles far more than we do at the present time. While rushes strewed upon the floor formed a sufficient carpet for even gentle ladies' feet; while the gallant knight's rough-and-ready toilet consisted in his plunging his head at daybreak into a bucket of cold water; while linen was coarse in manufacture, and food was prepared in such a manner as our modern cooks would call barbarous; while, in short, most of the refinements and delicacies which we have been accustomed by civilisation to regard almost in the light of necessaries, were still unknown, the goldsmith's and the jeweller's art was lavished upon many an object of household use on which even the most luxurious of modern Europeans would consider it the height of extravagance to employ it now. Not only the ecclesiastical furniture of the Middle Ages, but many of the domestic utensils of private life, were elaborated and enriched after a fashion which we should now only think suitable for a monarch's state crown, or at least for some splendid article of *vertu* intended perhaps to be put under a glass case and looked at with respect, but never used.

Now there are two points of view from which we may regard the possession of plate and jewellery. We may admire them for their intrinsic value, on account of the high price we paid for them, and the amount in sovereigns which they would fetch if sold again, or we may admire them for certain rare qualities of beauty, whether expressed in the nature of the material itself, or in the excellence of design and workmanship to which it has been subjected in manufacture. It is, I fear, chiefly to the former source that the general admiration of the goldsmith's and jeweller's art may in modern days be traced. If the multitudes who at the Great Exhibition of 1851 flocked to gaze with profound reverence at the Koh-i-noor had suddenly been told that the researches of science had proved it to be a piece of cut glass, valued at, say ten shillings, who would have stopped to waste his attention on so insignificant an object? Yet it was only at a certain hour in the day that this precious gem differed in outward appearance from a piece of glass. It is well known that the diamond, when subjected to a high temperature, may be reduced to the state of graphite. Let us suppose for an instant that anyone had discovered the secret of reversing that operation, how long would these gems remain fashionable ornaments? Not a single season. They would be at once and for ever banished from the heads and necks and stomachers of every court belle in Christendom. As it is, the imitation of diamonds is carried to such perfection in France that none but the most practised eye can distinguish the real jewel from its counterfeit. After this it would be absurd to suppose that the diamond is valued solely for its intrinsic beauty. The truth is we value it because it represents so much wealth.

For this reason the scientific cutting of precious stones, simply to ensure lustre by a certain refraction of light, and then only under certain conditions, would seem but a questionable advantage, especially when we remember that the shape thus obtained, at probably a great sacrifice of material, can always be assumed by the false gem with nearly as effective a result.   To have and to hold as one's own property one of the largest diamonds ever discovered, is no doubt a magnificent possession ; but in a purely artistic sense I prefer the original Koh-i-noor, worn on the arm of Runjeet Sing as he sat ' cross-legged in his golden chair, dressed in simple white, with a single string of huge pearls round his waist,' to the Koh-i-noor cut and pared down to mathematical symmetry by English lapidaries, with a loss of one-third of its weight.

It is to be feared that the possessors of diamonds in any quantity are, as a rule, not very likely to be influenced by suggestions which arise from the consideration of artistic taste ; yet I cannot refrain from pointing out what appears to me a great mistake made by ladies who insist on wearing a profusion of these gems clustered together either in the shape of what is called a tiara, or on any other part of their dress.   The true beauty of a diamond is best seen when it shines like a star from a dark ground on which, as in the firmament itself, it may have companions, but never in close association. A mass of diamonds grouped together in the form of a coronet, or, as we too frequently see them, in the ill-adopted form of a wreath of leaves and flowers, may produce a fitful *blaze* of light ; but so will tinsel or any other mean material used for a similar purpose. Such an effect as this is surely but a paltry one to aim at, and when it is obtained can only dazzle the eye and distract it from those charms which are popularly supposed to be enhanced by this mode of decoration. The subtle beauties of a fair woman's complexion, the modest lustre of an expressive eye, the delicate texture of soft wavy hair—are not these well nigh extinguished in the profuse glitter of surrounding brilliants ? Diamonds of any important size should be quite isolated, or if small should be arranged in small, distinct and geometrical groups on the ornament which they are intended to enrich.

It is lamentable to think how little real art is now displayed in the manufacture of jewellery, notwithstanding the enormous sums which are annually paid for it by private purchasers. Some time ago I visited the establishment of one of the leading West End firms, who very politely displayed their principal treasures for my inspection. I saw many articles of immense value, but I am sorry to say very few which reached anything like a high standard of taste in design. The workmanship seemed excellent : the gems were matched and cut and set with extraordinary precision and regularity, but the far more important qualities, which are indicative of the artist's hand— grace of form and composition — were generally wanting.

It would be unfair indeed to ascribe the dearth of good specimens to the indifference of manufacturers alone. It is a well-known fact that chaste and well-designed objects of jewellery—such as those, for instance, which have been reproduced from antique examples—*will not sell* in the English market. There is a demand for rare and expensive gems, and a ceaseless demand for showy designs, provided they are *novel*; but for that exquisite school of the goldsmith's art which Castellani laboured to revive in Rome, there is little popular appreciation in this country. At the shop which I have already mentioned I was shown a necklace of large single diamonds, the fancy of a particular customer, and valued at 20,000*l*. For a hundredth part of that sum a rich and beautiful work of art might have been produced and applied to the same purpose. But so long as people prefer the display of mere wealth to the encouragement of true principles in manufacture, we shall look vainly for improvement in the design of expensive jewellery.

I say expressly of *expensive* jewellery, for that which is of moderate price and exposed in ordinary shop windows is often in far better taste. The best designs are either directly copied or partially imitated from modern Roman work, the design of which is chiefly based on antique examples. They may be easily distinguished by the solid geometrical form which they assume, the groundwork of the gold being generally plain and unburnished, relieved by a delicate enrichment of the same material overlaid in thin corded lines. Bracelets, brooches, necklaces (with pendants in the form of the ancient *bulla*), earrings, armlets, &c., of this kind may be bought in many of the shops at the West End of London. The International Exhibition of 1872 contained some excellent examples of this class produced by British jewellers.

But if we wish to find specimens of really artistic jewellery, we must seek them in the museums, for they are not the productions of the present age; or if of the present age, certainly not of this country. At South Kensington alone there are countless treasures from which, if they were properly studied, might be formed a standard of taste far higher than that of our own day.   It is not only from the much prized *cinque-cento* work of France and Italy—beautiful as most of it is—that we may learn a lesson.   Even the rudely-made peasant trinkets of Russia, the unskilled manufactures of central India, the quaint and early devices of Rhenish Byzantine artists are all infinitely superior to what we have made or invented in the way of jewellery during our boasted nineteenth century.*

In the east cloister of the South Court at the Kensington Museum were, not long ago, some cases of Oriental jewellery lent by Sir R. N. Hamilton, and well worth inspection.   Those specimens are for the most part of Bhopal and Indore work, remarkable not only for extreme simplicity, but for an elegance and appropriateness of design which our jewellers would do well to imitate.   Amongst others was a throat ornament or flat necklace, composed of little tablets of gold about three-quarters of an inch long and three-eighths broad, divided transversely into three panels, each containing a ruby.   These panels alternate with

* Some of the Algerine trinkets, lately sold in London, of white metal, decorated with beads in imitation of coral and turquoise, are really admirable in design and worthy of the best periods of ancient art-manufacture. They are hand-made specimens of native work.   If our jewellers would only reproduce them, using silver and real stones for their material, they would be doing good service in the cause of household taste.

a double row of four seed pearls, disposed so as to
occupy about the same space as the adjoining ornament throughout the length of the necklace (about
seven inches), except that at each extremity of the

band the panels, instead of being oblong, are trefoil
shaped. To these extremities are attached a small
silken cord of crimson colour, whipped round with gold
thread, which serves to fasten this ornament round
the neck of the wearer.

In the same case was a kind of fillet for the head,

composed of small uncut rubies and other precious
stones inclosed in hexagonal and plain oval settings,
and alternating with seed pearls in several rows. The
last row is decorated with little pendants, each of which
terminates with a tiny emerald. Another ingenious
and pretty ornament, also intended to be worn in the
hair, was one composed of seven gold pendants, six set
with emeralds and rubies, and one with pearl clusters,
attached by seven gold chains to a chased link. The

pendants all differ slightly in form—some are quatrefoil, some are hexagons, some are heart-shaped; and it
is to be observed that in this Indian work generally,
when gems are introduced in the design, they are either
left completely uncut (as when they are used for pendants without setting), or they are only just trimmed
sufficiently to make them handy for the manner in
which they are to be held. The notion of grinding and
paring gems down to a uniform size for a necklace or
bracelet is a thoroughly modern and European one,

and helps to render our jewellery formal and uninteresting. In old and Oriental work we find the collet or rim which is to hold the jewel accommodated to the shape of the latter. Gems which are intended to be placed in a row, or to balance each other in design, are matched pretty nearly in size, but never with scrupulous accuracy. The result is, that the collets all vary a little in outline; and this, so far from interfering with the general effect, seems to me to add greatly to its interest, for such irregularity is a direct evidence of manual work, whereas fashionable jewellery of our own day looks as if it had been made, and indeed is to a great extent made, by machinery. Why our lapidaries should be obliged to waste time, and labour, and precious material, in order to make two little stones precisely like each other, is a mystery which the genius of modern taste can alone explain.

Among other objects in the same collection was a set of eleven little golden tablets, measuring about an inch and a quarter across, and about one-sixteenth of an inch thick. They are of octagonal and oval shapes, chased into grotesque groups of men and animals, and surrounded by a delicate leaf border. The interstices between the figures are cut away, and this open work thus formed appears relieved upon a ground of emerald-green foil or enamel. Minute as the details

of this design are, they are executed with great spirit and knowledge of drawing. It is a peculiarity of all good conventional ornament, whether in low relief or in superficial decoration, that the space which it occupies is generally found to balance in equal proportions the space of the ground on which it is relieved. This condition has been admirably observed in the work to which I refer. The tablets appear to have formed links or compartments in a necklace or waistband.

Very different in style, but designed with great *naïveté* and picturesque effect, were the examples of Russian jewellery lately exhibited in the South Court at Kensington. The date to which they are ascribed is that of the seventeenth century, but they have all the character of much earlier work when compared with the taste which prevailed in more civilised parts of Europe during that period. These specimens consist of earrings, neckchains, pectoral crosses, devotional tablets, &c., simple in general form, and boldly but artistically treated. Twisted gold and silver wire is

frequently introduced as a decorative feature. One of
the crosses is of silver gilt, ornamented with green
enamel in a foliated *cloisonné* pattern. In the centre is

a garnet, and at each end of the cross is a turquoise.
Another good example of this class is a small spherical
pendant of silver-gilt filagree work, about an inch in
diameter, set with turquoises and garnets. In this

Russian jewellery, as in the Indian work, the setting of
the precious stones continually varies with their shape,
and is no doubt what London modern jewellers would
call rude and clumsy. French art of the same period,
and even of a much earlier date, is, on the contrary,
elegant and minute in its finish. A charming necklace
of gold filagree work, ornamented with rosettes in white
enamel, and set with emeralds and rubies, may be seen
in one of the flat cases of this court. It appears to have
been purchased by the Kensington authorities for nine
guineas. It would have been cheap at double that
sum. Close by this jewel was a pendant of enamelled
gold, set with emeralds and sapphires.* In its centre
is a little onyx cameo representing a profile bust of the
youthful Hercules in relief, and probably copied from
the antique. The design of the goldsmith's work is
presumed to be Italian, and of the sixteenth century—
perhaps rather too late in it for purity of mere decorative form, but the skill and execution of the work are
admirable. An exquisite example of Rhenish-Byzan-
tine design (from the Soltykoff collection) appears in
the adjoining case. It is a crucifix of cedar wood

---

* The position of some of these specimens may have been changed
since this was written, but those which belong to the permanent collection
could no doubt be easily found and identified.

XXX

Locket and Necklace executed by Howell & James,
from a design by Sir Digby Wyatt.

coated with thin plate of beaten gold. This is decorated with delicate cords of gold-twist laid on in a relieved pattern, and *plaques* of enamel occur at each extremity of the cross. The figure, of walrus ivory, seems

hardly equal to the rest in merit of design. The above, of course, are only a very few out of a host of objects at Kensington the description of which might serve to illustrate principles essential to this department of ' household taste.' Mr. Beresford Hope's collection alone (or rather that portion of it which is lent to the Museum for exhibition) contains treasures of art in connection with manufacture which no one can examine without profit, but which it would be impossible to enumerate here.

Among the specimens of modern work, a silver bracelet damascened in gold with a *niello* ground, manufactured by Mons. J. Roucon, of Paris, and the very successful copies of ancient Irish brooches, executed by two Dublin firms, Messrs. West and Messrs. Waterhouse, are well worth notice. They at least show us that there is no lack of mechanical skill or ingenuity in this branch of industrial art at the present day. The real deficiency lies in the want of appreciation on the part of the public. As soon as this appreciation is felt and good designs are in common request, there is no reason to doubt that they will be supplied.

On Plates XXX. and XXXI. are engraved specimens of modern jewellery executed by Messrs. Howell and James for the International Exhibition of 1872. The first is a locket forming part of a handsome *parure* designed by the late Sir Digby Wyatt. It is executed in gold, modelled in low relief, and set with pearls and diamonds. The locket, earring, and

XXXI

Locket, Ear-ring, and Bracelet executed by Howell & James,
from a design by Charles L. Eastlake.

bracelet on Plate XXXI. are from my own design, and consist of cameos held in a gold setting enriched with jewels, seed pearls, and enamelled work.

I cannot conclude this chapter without calling the reader's attention to the inestimable advantages and opportunity for improvement of national style in this and almost every other branch of manufacture, which this country possesses in the South Kensington Museum. However much opinions may differ as to the system of instruction in design hitherto adopted in that Department, there can be no doubt that the truly magnificent collection of objects assembled there, and the facility afforded to students who may desire to inspect and study them, reflect the highest credit upon the authorities entrusted with its care. By such means, the art-workman, his employer, and the public whose encouragement and patronage are necessary to both, may learn that which alone can rescue English manufacture from its recent degradation, viz. :—the formation of a sound taste.

Chapter XII.

PLATE AND CUTLERY.

 WELL-APPOINTED dinner-table is one of the triumphs of an English housewife's domestic care. That the cloth shall be of fine and snow-white damask; that the decanters and wine-glasses shall be delicate in form and of purest quality; that the silver shall look as bright and spotless as when it first came wrapped in tissue-paper from the silversmith's; that the *épergne* shall be filled with choicest flowers—these are points which she will consider of as much importance as the dainty skill of the cook's art itself. Indeed, the general effect of a rich dinner service, or of a well-arranged buffet, contributes a more picturesque element than is apparent elsewhere, to the appointment of a modern household. But if we examine in detail the various articles which, under the general name of 'plate,' form this display, we shall find that they depend for their attraction on richness of material rather than on sound principles of design.

A sense of mere *prettiness* in decorative art belongs in some sort to our very earliest instincts. A mere baby will crow with pleasure at the sight of a gold watch or any glittering object, and try to clutch it with eager hands. In childhood the most elaborate and richly painted toys are preferred to those of a simpler kind ; and, indeed, to a maturer but still natural taste the brilliant colour and complex form of manufactured objects are generally agreeable, without reference to the purpose for which such objects were designed.

The use of colour—applied by the process known as enamelling, and once so valuable an enrichment of metal work—has been long out of vogue in the manufacture of plate. The same may be said to a great extent of damascened, *niello,* and engraved ornament. A base imitation of the old *repoussé* work lent a vulgar kind of richness to silver teapots and cream-jugs designed in the once all-prevalent but objectionable taste of the Louis XV. period ; but a large proportion of modern plate is stamped in patterns which have no more artistic quality than the ornaments of a wedding-cake. Take, for instance, the ordinary 'fiddle pattern' fork ; can anything be more senseless than the way in which modifications of that form are deco-rated—now with a raised moulding at its edge, now with an outline of beads, now with what is called a 'shell,' but what is really a bad copy of the Greek honeysuckle ornament, at the end of its handle, now with a rococo scroll or a representation of *natural* flowers in low relief on its surface ? All these patterns are dignified by fine names, such as the 'Albert,' the 'Brunswick,' the 'Rose,' the 'Lily.' They are repro-duced over and over again at Birmingham and else-where. People buy them because there is nothing else of the kind to be had ; but there is no more *art* in their design than there is in that of a modern bed-post. Compare them with the charming examples of antique silver which may still be seen in the windows of a curiosity shop, and observe how much we have retrograded in this department of manufacture.*

Now I am not going to recommend the re-introduc-tion of what were called 'Apostle' spoons for ordinary use. The chased figure of a saint or of a ship in

---

* Since these lines were written Messrs. John Yates & Son of Pritchett Street, Birmingham, have commissioned me to prepare a series of designs for plated goods intended for ordinary table use. Some of these articles are now in course of manufacture, and I hope in a future edition of this book to engrave some specimens of the work.

full sail (a favourite termination for the fork or spoon handle of olden days) may not be the most convenient thing for the fair fingers of a lady to hold at dinner; and it must be confessed that the bowls were wider and more capacious than we require for that infini-

tesimal portion of soup which is served out to each guest at a modern banquet. I merely mean that the *spirit* with which this old plate was designed is extinct in our modern silver. It would be quite possible to fashion graceful spoons and forks which should also suit the most fastidious notions of convenience. A modern fork looks top-heavy because it has four prongs. Three prongs were once considered sufficient, and with three alone the fork would gain in lightness and appearance. Again, the stem of the old spoon was a delicate rod,

sometimes twisted and sometimes square in section. It is now flat and heavy, requiring nearly twice as much metal in its manufacture, and therefore materially increasing the cost of silver plate. It may indeed be desirable, for the sake of convenience in handling, to keep the upper end of the stem flat, but in other respects the old shape seems preferable, and is certainly less expensive. In fact, all old plate of the best period was infinitely lighter in weight than our own. Its chief value consisted in its design; whereas that of the present day can but be estimated in ounces. It is perhaps for this reason that modern silversmiths prefer to load their plate with heavy *raised* ornament, instead of adopting the delicate *incised* patterns once in vogue.

In the whole range of art-manufacture there are no more deplorable examples of taste than the silver side-dishes, soup-tureens, cruet-stands, salvers, and candle-sticks of the nineteenth century. The most extra-vagant forms are enriched with ornament, which is either a caricature of Renaissance detail, or simply feeble representations of natural form.

I have an illustrated catalogue of electro-plated goods before me at the present moment, in which a fish-slice is shown decorated with an engraved *land-scape,* surrounded by acanthus scrolls. Further on I find a rose, a tulip, and an apple respectively doing duty as the handle of a tea-pot lid, and an egg-stand designed in imitation of a wicker-basket. As for the butter-cooler, it is, of course, surmounted by that inevitable cow which fashion has consecrated for our breakfast tables, in order, I presume, that we may never forget the source and origin of one of the most useful articles of daily food.

It is by no means easy to offer suggestions which should guide an ordinary taste in the choice of such objects as these. Perhaps the soundest advice to give would be that which is based on common sense. In an age of debased design at least, the simplest style will be the best. Choose a pure outlined form rather than that which is defined by a dozen varying curves. Round silver dishes and salvers are preferable to those of an oval or square shape for many reasons, and especially on account of the mode in which such articles are manufactured. Richly moulded edges are, for a like reason, inappropriate ; moreover, in precious metal they necessarily increase the cost, and in plated goods they are liable to be rubbed and look shabby. Vessels of silver should be composed of thin plate, and the best means of decorating them is either by piercing the metal with open-work ornament, by engraving conventional (i.e., non-naturalistic) surface-patterns, or by *repoussé* decoration, which consists in beating out the silver from inside into bosses and arabesques. The latter mode, if well executed, is of course the most expensive. All articles of plate which represent in miniature objects of a different material—as barrels, tubs, and baskets—should be avoided. There was a time when it was thought tasteful to let every knick-knack for the table assume an appearance which utterly belied its real purpose. Some of my readers may remember the little gilt Cupid wheeling a barrow full of salt, which once appeared in many an English dining-room, and I have often been surprised that no ingenious Sheffield designer has yet adapted the Martyrs' Memorial for a pepper-castor.

The substitution of electro-plate for real silver is now so common in households where the latter would be regarded as a superfluous luxury, that the sternest advocate of true principles in art-manufacture would scarcely require an apology for its use. The fact is, that even in the best ages of design some such expedient has been practised, and therefore has long since ceased to be a deception. In the case of a dinner service, there is sufficient excuse for its adoption in the fact that steel forks and pewter spoons are not pleasant things to eat with. If a coating of silver meets that objection, surely it is desirable to use it. We must remember that in this, as in other departments of 'household taste,' the intrinsic value of the material is of minor importance to the mode in which it is fashioned ; and so far as the interests of art are concerned it is better to possess a copper gilt flagon of a good design than a modern 'trophy cup' of twice its weight in gold. If the pieces of 'presentation plate' which we are invited to inspect at silversmiths' before they are sent off to their worthy possessors were only entrusted to competent designers, we might hope for something better than the everlasting palm-trees, camels and equestrian groups which are now allowed to symbolise both the taste and the gratitude of a generous public. In such objects as those to which I refer, the art-workman does little more than model more or less correctly after nature. This, as I have already endeavoured to show, is imitation, but not *design* in the artistic sense of the word. Both Benvenuto Cellini and Holbein were admirable draughtsmen ; both were thoroughly acquainted with the proportions of the human figure ; but, though they lived in an age when decorative art had lost its early simplicity, neither of them forgot its conditions so far as to let a naturalistic treatment of animal form predominate in their designs for plate.

To return, however, to the more ordinary articles of table use, there seems but little from a practical point of view that could be suggested by way of improvement for modern cutlery. Yet the shape of an English dinner-knife, with its flat bone handle and straight round-topped blade, is one of the most uninteresting that could be devised for the purpose. The old-fashioned knife-handle was gently curved, so that it might be grasped with more convenience, as in the annexed example (of damascened steel) from the South Kensington Museum, and it is a remarkable evidence of the inappropriateness of modern manufacture that while we have bent the stems of our spoons which are intended to be held lightly between the fingers, we have reduced the outline of the knife-handle, which requires a firmer hold, to a simple parallelogram.

Again, as regards material, a white bone handle looks well enough while new and clean, but the yellowish colour which it acquires by constant use is not pleasant. It might be difficult and expensive to revive the manufacture of 'shagreen' for knife handles; but if made of bone, there seems no reason why they should not be stained, as was once the fashion. Dark wooden handles, studded with flat steel ornaments, were much used, I believe, in the last century, and certainly surpassed those of our own day in design. The old system of pinning the steel shank of the knife through the side of its handle has been renewed of late years—and with good reason, for in no other way can the two be properly secured together. A very slight curve in the length of the blade might be introduced with advantage, and this, for practical reasons, should be on the upper rather than on the lower edge. Foreign table-knives often have an *angular* end to the blade. The principal objection to this form lies in the danger which might ensue if a knife accidentally fell with its point downwards. It was perhaps on this account that the blades of some old-fashioned table-knives terminated with a round wafer-shaped top, like the butter-knife which may still be seen in use. A more probable reason, however, for that particular form lies in the fact that, down to the period of the last century, the table-knife was sometimes allowed to do duty for a spoon. Happily, that inelegant custom is extinct in our own day.

In the accompanying woodcut are given specimens of a small knife and fork, with carved wooden handles, from the South Kensington Museum. The style of execution is somewhat rude, but the nature and general proportions of the design are admirably adapted for the purpose. The illustration is about one-third less than the real size.

Mother-of-pearl handled knives and forks for dessert may now be bought at a very reasonable price, and are far more agreeable to the touch, as well as in appearance, than those made entirely of silver or plated metal, which are generally of very poor design. Mother-of-pearl, moreover, does not discolour with age, like bone or ivory.

A slight improvement may be noticed in the recent design of some small articles of table service, as mustard-pots, salt-cellars, and cruet-stands, but as a rule they are far inferior, both as regards taste and execution, to those which were manufactured not only at the best time, but early in the last century. Indeed, if I might venture to offer any direct advice of the kind which one constantly sees associated with catchpenny advertisements, and addressed to ' persons about to furnish,' I should suggest their buying plate, not at the magnificent emporium of Messrs. So-and-so—where the eye is perplexed by a hundred and fifty pretentious vulgarities—but rather at some of the old jewellery-shops in Hanway Street or Wardour Street, in which articles of old silver are still sold, far better in design, and at a cost rarely exceeding that which is paid for modern plate of the same intrinsic value. Some of the mediæval metal-workers have, it is true, attempted to revive the ancient taste and dignity of the silversmith's art; but while they charge for their goods a price which is at least double that of the ordinary trade, we can hardly expect them to be patronised by the public at large. A good simple design ought not to involve more labour in execution than a bad elaborate design, supposing both to be equally well executed ; and the execution of ordinary ware is at least good enough for all practical purposes.

The future success of art-manufacture in England must, of course, depend in a great measure on the taste of the public for whom it is supplied; but it is difficult to see how that taste is to be thoroughly and popularly reformed until manufacturers begin to educate it, by the production and display of goods which will bear the test of sound criticism. Museums and exhibitions of art treasures are useful in familiarising the eye with the appearance of objects which illustrate excellence of ancient skill. But it must be remembered that such objects are usually articles of luxury, which at any period would lie beyond the reach of ordinary means, and which in many instances were applied to some purpose that has long since fallen into disuse. In examining them, we are apt to forget that our fore-fathers were not all people of unlimited wealth, who could afford jewelled caskets, costly embroidery, richly carved cabinet-work and plate, which would fetch ten times its weight in gold and silver.

In those early days there were, as now, households in which economy was an object. Pots and pans, wooden trenchers and three-legged stools — articles, in short, far more humble in make and material than those which increased commercial prosperity has given to our present homes—were then required, produced, and sold at a moderate price. But it was not because they were cheap that they were necessarily ugly or ill-fashioned. That contemptible kind of workmanship which is at once slovenly and tasteless because it may be showy and cheap was not then in demand. The rich, indeed, spent more money, both on dress and objects of general luxury, than at the present day ; but such furniture as befitted the habits of ordinary citizens and country gentlefolks of that date was found in the homes of the middle classes more than two hundred years ago ; and wherever it existed, we may be sure it was deftly and honestly made. Those examples of ancient handicraft which have reached our own time may well put to shame the efforts of modern smiths and cabinet-makers who work like machines, while their ancestors worked like artists and practical men.

It would be absurd, however, to suppose that English capacity has deteriorated in the same pro-portion as English taste. Our artisans have as much intelligence as ever ; it only wants proper direction and employment. At present both master and man are so accustomed, from their youth up, to false principles of design and execution, that it requires some stern teaching and no little patience to lead them back to their proper groove of work. Meanwhile, the public must do their part. If they will insist on the perpetuation of pretentious shams—if they will prefer a cheap and tawdry effect to legitimate and straightforward manufacture—no reform can possibly be expected. But if they encourage that sound and healthy taste which alone is found allied with conscientious labour, whether in the workshop or the factory, then we may hope to see revived the ancient glory of those industrial arts which, while they derive a certain interest from tradition, should owe their highest perfection to civilised skill.

INDEX.

.

A CATALOG OF SELECTED
DOVER BOOKS
IN ALL FIELDS OF INTEREST

A CATALOG OF SELECTED DOVER

BOOKS IN ALL FIELDS OF INTEREST

DRAWINGS OF REMBRANDT, edited by Seymour Slive. Updated Lippmann, Hofstede de Groot edition, with definitive scholarly apparatus. All portraits, biblical sketches, landscapes, nudes. Oriental figures, classical studies, together with selection of work by followers. 550 illustrations. Total of 630pp. 9⅛ × 12¼.
21485-0, 21486-9 Pa., Two-vol. set $29.90

GHOST AND HORROR STORIES OF AMBROSE BIERCE, Ambrose Bierce. 24 tales vividly imagined, strangely prophetic, and decades ahead of their time in technical skill: "The Damned Thing," "An Inhabitant of Carcosa," "The Eyes of the Panther," "Moxon's Master," and 20 more. 199pp. 5⅜ × 8½. 20767-6 Pa. $4.95

ETHICAL WRITINGS OF MAIMONIDES, Maimonides. Most significant ethical works of great medieval sage, newly translated for utmost precision, readability. Laws Concerning Character Traits, Eight Chapters, more. 192pp. 5⅜ × 8½.
24522-5 Pa. $4.50

THE EXPLORATION OF THE COLORADO RIVER AND ITS CANYONS, J. W. Powell. Full text of Powell's 1,000-mile expedition down the fabled Colorado in 1869. Superb account of terrain, geology, vegetation, Indians, famine, mutiny, treacherous rapids, mighty canyons, during exploration of last unknown part of continental U.S. 400pp. 5⅜ × 8½. 20094-9 Pa. $7.95

HISTORY OF PHILOSOPHY, Julián Marías. Clearest one-volume history on the market. Every major philosopher and dozens of others, to Existentialism and later. 505pp. 5⅜ × 8½. 21739-6 Pa. $9.95

ALL ABOUT LIGHTNING, Martin A. Uman. Highly readable non-technical survey of nature and causes of lightning, thunderstorms, ball lightning, St. Elmo's Fire, much more. Illustrated. 192pp. 5⅜ × 8½. 25237-X Pa. $5.95

SAILING ALONE AROUND THE WORLD, Captain Joshua Slocum. First man to sail around the world, alone, in small boat. One of great feats of seamanship told in delightful manner. 67 illustrations. 294pp. 5⅜ × 8½. 20326-3 Pa. $4.95

LETTERS AND NOTES ON THE MANNERS, CUSTOMS AND CONDI-TIONS OF THE NORTH AMERICAN INDIANS, George Catlin. Classic account of life among Plains Indians: ceremonies, hunt, warfare, etc. 312 plates. 572pp. of text. 6⅛ × 9¼. 22118-0, 22119-9, Pa. Two-vol. set $17.90

ALASKA: The Harriman Expedition, 1899, John Burroughs, John Muir, et al. Informative, engrossing accounts of two-month, 9,000-mile expedition. Native peoples, wildlife, forests, geography, salmon industry, glaciers, more. Profusely illustrated. 240 black-and-white line drawings. 124 black-and-white photographs. 3 maps. Index. 576pp. 5⅜ × 8½. 25109-8 Pa. $11.95

THE BOOK OF BEASTS: Being a Translation from a Latin Bestiary of the Twelfth Century, T. H. White. Wonderful catalog real and fanciful beasts: manticore, griffin, phoenix, amphivius, jaculus, many more. White's witty erudite commentary on scientific, historical aspects. Fascinating glimpse of medieval mind. Illustrated. 296pp. 5⅜ × 8¼. (Available in U.S. only) 24609-4 Pa. $6.95

FRANK LLOYD WRIGHT: ARCHITECTURE AND NATURE With 160 Illustrations, Donald Hoffmann. Profusely illustrated study of influence of nature—especially prairie—on Wright's designs for Fallingwater, Robie House, Guggenheim Museum, other masterpieces. 96pp. 9¼ × 10¾. 25098-9 Pa. $8.95

FRANK LLOYD WRIGHT'S FALLINGWATER, Donald Hoffmann. Wright's famous waterfall house: planning and construction of organic idea. History of site, owners, Wright's personal involvement. Photographs of various stages of building. Preface by Edgar Kaufmann, Jr. 100 illustrations. 112pp. 9¼ × 10.
23671-4 Pa. $8.95

YEARS WITH FRANK LLOYD WRIGHT: Apprentice to Genius, Edgar Tafel. Insightful memoir by a former apprentice presents a revealing portrait of Wright the man, the inspired teacher, the greatest American architect. 372 black-and-white illustrations. Preface. Index. vi + 228pp. 8¼ × 11. 24801-1 Pa. $10.95

THE STORY OF KING ARTHUR AND HIS KNIGHTS, Howard Pyle. Enchanting version of King Arthur fable has delighted generations with imaginative narratives of exciting adventures and unforgettable illustrations by the author. 41 illustrations. xviii + 313pp. 6⅛ × 9¼. 21445-1 Pa. $6.95

THE GODS OF THE EGYPTIANS, E. A. Wallis Budge. Thorough coverage of numerous gods of ancient Egypt by foremost Egyptologist. Information on evolution of cults, rites and gods; the cult of Osiris; the Book of the Dead and its rites; the sacred animals and birds; Heaven and Hell; and more. 956pp. 6⅛ × 9¼.
22055-9, 22056-7 Pa., Two-vol. set $21.90

A THEOLOGICO-POLITICAL TREATISE, Benedict Spinoza. Also contains unfinished *Political Treatise*. Great classic on religious liberty, theory of government on common consent. R. Elwes translation. Total of 421pp. 5⅜ × 8½.
20249-6 Pa. $7.95

INCIDENTS OF TRAVEL IN CENTRAL AMERICA, CHIAPAS, AND YUCATAN, John L. Stephens. Almost single-handed discovery of Maya culture; exploration of ruined cities, monuments, temples; customs of Indians. 115 drawings. 892pp. 5⅜ × 8½. 22404-X, 22405-8 Pa., Two-vol. set $15.90

LOS CAPRICHOS, Francisco Goya. 80 plates of wild, grotesque monsters and caricatures. Prado manuscript included. 183pp. 6⅞ × 9⅜. 22384-1 Pa. $5.95

AUTOBIOGRAPHY: The Story of My Experiments with Truth, Mohandas K. Gandhi. Not hagiography, but Gandhi in his own words. Boyhood, legal studies, purification, the growth of the Satyagraha (nonviolent protest) movement. Critical, inspiring work of the man who freed India. 480pp. 5⅜ × 8½. (Available in U.S. only)
24593-4 Pa. $6.95

ILLUSTRATED DICTIONARY OF HISTORIC ARCHITECTURE, edited by Cyril M. Harris. Extraordinary compendium of clear, concise definitions for over 5,000 important architectural terms complemented by over 2,000 line drawings. Covers full spectrum of architecture from ancient ruins to 20th-century Modernism. Preface. 592pp. 7½ × 9⅝. 24444-X Pa. $15.95

THE NIGHT BEFORE CHRISTMAS, Clement Moore. Full text, and woodcuts from original 1848 book. Also critical, historical material. 19 illustrations. 40pp. 4⅝ × 6. 22797-9 Pa. $2.50

THE LESSON OF JAPANESE ARCHITECTURE: 165 Photographs, Jiro Harada. Memorable gallery of 165 photographs taken in the 1930's of exquisite Japanese homes of the well-to-do and historic buildings. 13 line diagrams. 192pp. 8⅜ × 11¼. 24778-3 Pa. $10.95

THE AUTOBIOGRAPHY OF CHARLES DARWIN AND SELECTED LETTERS, edited by Francis Darwin. The fascinating life of eccentric genius composed of an intimate memoir by Darwin (intended for his children); commentary by his son, Francis; hundreds of fragments from notebooks, journals, papers; and letters to and from Lyell, Hooker, Huxley, Wallace and Henslow. xi + 365pp. 5⅜ × 8. 20479-0 Pa. $6.95

WONDERS OF THE SKY: Observing Rainbows, Comets, Eclipses, the Stars and Other Phenomena, Fred Schaaf. Charming, easy-to-read poetic guide to all manner of celestial events visible to the naked eye. Mock suns, glories, Belt of Venus, more. Illustrated. 299pp. 5¼ × 8¼. 24402-4 Pa. $7.95

BURNHAM'S CELESTIAL HANDBOOK, Robert Burnham, Jr. Thorough guide to the stars beyond our solar system. Exhaustive treatment. Alphabetical by constellation: Andromeda to Cetus in Vol. 1; Chamaeleon to Orion in Vol. 2; and Pavo to Vulpecula in Vol. 3. Hundreds of illustrations. Index in Vol. 3. 2,000pp. 6⅛ × 9¼. 23567-X, 23568-8, 23673-0 Pa., Three-vol. set $41.85

STAR NAMES: Their Lore and Meaning, Richard Hinckley Allen. Fascinating history of names various cultures have given to constellations and literary and folkloristic uses that have been made of stars. Indexes to subjects. Arabic and Greek names. Biblical references. Bibliography. 563pp. 5⅜ × 8½. 21079-0 Pa. $8.95

THIRTY YEARS THAT SHOOK PHYSICS: The Story of Quantum Theory, George Gamow. Lucid, accessible introduction to influential theory of energy and matter. Careful explanations of Dirac's anti-particles, Bohr's model of the atom, much more. 12 plates. Numerous drawings. 240pp. 5⅜ × 8½. 24895-X Pa. $5.95

CHINESE DOMESTIC FURNITURE IN PHOTOGRAPHS AND MEASURED DRAWINGS, Gustav Ecke. A rare volume, now affordably priced for antique collectors, furniture buffs and art historians. Detailed review of styles ranging from early Shang to late Ming. Unabridged republication. 161 black-and-white drawings, photos. Total of 224pp. 8⅜ × 11¼. (Available in U.S. only) 25171-3 Pa. $13.95

VINCENT VAN GOGH: A Biography, Julius Meier-Graefe. Dynamic, penetrating study of artist's life, relationship with brother, Theo, painting techniques, travels, more. Readable, engrossing. 160pp. 5⅜ × 8½. (Available in U.S. only) 25253-1 Pa. $4.95

HOW TO WRITE, Gertrude Stein. Gertrude Stein claimed anyone could understand her unconventional writing—here are clues to help. Fascinating improvisations, language experiments, explanations illuminate Stein's craft and the art of writing. Total of 414pp. 4⅝ × 6⅜. 23144-5 Pa. $6.95

ADVENTURES AT SEA IN THE GREAT AGE OF SAIL: Five Firsthand Narratives, edited by Elliot Snow. Rare true accounts of exploration, whaling, shipwreck, fierce natives, trade, shipboard life, more. 33 illustrations. Introduction. 353pp. 5⅜ × 8½. 25177-2 Pa. $8.95

THE HERBAL OR GENERAL HISTORY OF PLANTS, John Gerard. Classic descriptions of about 2,850 plants—with over 2,700 illustrations—includes Latin and English names, physical descriptions, varieties, time and place of growth, more. 2,706 illustrations. xlv + 1,678pp. 8½ × 12¼. 23147-X Cloth. $75.00

DOROTHY AND THE WIZARD IN OZ, L. Frank Baum. Dorothy and the Wizard visit the center of the Earth, where people are vegetables, glass houses grow and Oz characters reappear. Classic sequel to *Wizard of Oz*. 256pp. 5⅜ × 8. 24714-7 Pa. $5.95

SONGS OF EXPERIENCE: Facsimile Reproduction with 26 Plates in Full Color, William Blake. This facsimile of Blake's original "Illuminated Book" reproduces 26 full-color plates from a rare 1826 edition. Includes "The Tyger," "London," "Holy Thursday," and other immortal poems. 26 color plates. Printed text of poems. 48pp. 5¼ × 7. 24636-1 Pa. $3.95

SONGS OF INNOCENCE, William Blake. The first and most popular of Blake's famous "Illuminated Books," in a facsimile edition reproducing all 31 brightly colored plates. Additional printed text of each poem. 64pp. 5¼ × 7. 22764-2 Pa. $3.95

PRECIOUS STONES, Max Bauer. Classic, thorough study of diamonds, rubies, emeralds, garnets, etc.: physical character, occurrence, properties, use, similar topics. 20 plates, 8 in color. 94 figures. 659pp. 6⅛ × 9¼. 21910-0, 21911-9 Pa., Two-vol. set $15.90

ENCYCLOPEDIA OF VICTORIAN NEEDLEWORK, S. F. A. Caulfeild and Blanche Saward. Full, precise descriptions of stitches, techniques for dozens of needlecrafts—most exhaustive reference of its kind. Over 800 figures. Total of 679pp. 8⅛ × 11. Two volumes.   Vol. 1 22800-2 Pa. $11.95
Vol. 2 22801-0 Pa. $11.95

THE MARVELOUS LAND OF OZ, L. Frank Baum. Second Oz book, the Scarecrow and Tin Woodman are back with hero named Tip, Oz magic. 136 illustrations. 287pp. 5⅜ × 8½. 20692-0 Pa. $5.95

WILD FOWL DECOYS, Joel Barber. Basic book on the subject, by foremost authority and collector. Reveals history of decoy making and rigging, place in American culture, different kinds of decoys, how to make them, and how to use them. 140 plates. 156pp. 7⅞ × 10¾. 20011-6 Pa. $8.95

HISTORY OF LACE, Mrs. Bury Palliser. Definitive, profusely illustrated chronicle of lace from earliest times to late 19th century. Laces of Italy, Greece, England, France, Belgium, etc. Landmark of needlework scholarship. 266 illustrations. 672pp. 6⅛ × 9¼. 24742-2 Pa. $14.95

ILLUSTRATED GUIDE TO SHAKER FURNITURE, Robert Meader. All furniture and appurtenances, with much on unknown local styles. 235 photos. 146pp. 9 × 12. 22819-3 Pa. $8.95

WHALE SHIPS AND WHALING: A Pictorial Survey, George Francis Dow. Over 200 vintage engravings, drawings, photographs of barks, brigs, cutters, other vessels. Also harpoons, lances, whaling guns, many other artifacts. Comprehensive text by foremost authority. 207 black-and-white illustrations. 288pp. 6 × 9. 24808-9 Pa. $9.95

THE BERTRAMS, Anthony Trollope. Powerful portrayal of blind self-will and thwarted ambition includes one of Trollope's most heartrending love stories. 497pp. 5⅜ × 8½. 25119-5 Pa. $9.95

ADVENTURES WITH A HAND LENS, Richard Headstrom. Clearly written guide to observing and studying flowers and grasses, fish scales, moth and insect wings, egg cases, buds, feathers, seeds, leaf scars, moss, molds, ferns, common crystals, etc.—all with an ordinary, inexpensive magnifying glass. 209 exact line drawings aid in your discoveries. 220pp. 5⅜ × 8½. 23330-8 Pa. $4.95

RODIN ON ART AND ARTISTS, Auguste Rodin. Great sculptor's candid, wide-ranging comments on meaning of art; great artists; relation of sculpture to poetry, painting, music; philosophy of life, more. 76 superb black-and-white illustrations of Rodin's sculpture, drawings and prints. 119pp. 8⅜ × 11¼. 24487-3 Pa. $7.95

FIFTY CLASSIC FRENCH FILMS, 1912–1982: A Pictorial Record, Anthony Slide. Memorable stills from Grand Illusion, Beauty and the Beast, Hiroshima, Mon Amour, many more. Credits, plot synopses, reviews, etc. 160pp. 8¼ × 11. 25256-6 Pa. $11.95

THE PRINCIPLES OF PSYCHOLOGY, William James. Famous long course complete, unabridged. Stream of thought, time perception, memory, experimental methods; great work decades ahead of its time. 94 figures. 1,391pp. 5⅜ × 8½. 20381-6, 20382-4 Pa., Two-vol. set $23.90

BODIES IN A BOOKSHOP, R. T. Campbell. Challenging mystery of blackmail and murder with ingenious plot and superbly drawn characters. In the best tradition of British suspense fiction. 192pp. 5⅜ × 8½. 24720-1 Pa. $4.95

CALLAS: PORTRAIT OF A PRIMA DONNA, George Jellinek. Renowned commentator on the musical scene chronicles incredible career and life of the most controversial, fascinating, influential operatic personality of our time. 64 black-and-white photographs. 416pp. 5⅜ × 8¼. 25047-4 Pa. $8.95

GEOMETRY, RELATIVITY AND THE FOURTH DIMENSION, Rudolph Rucker. Exposition of fourth dimension, concepts of relativity as Flatland characters continue adventures. Popular, easily followed yet accurate, profound. 141 illustrations. 133pp. 5⅜ × 8½. 23400-2 Pa. $4.95

HOUSEHOLD STORIES BY THE BROTHERS GRIMM, with pictures by Walter Crane. 53 classic stories—Rumpelstiltskin, Rapunzel, Hansel and Gretel, the Fisherman and his Wife, Snow White, Tom Thumb, Sleeping Beauty, Cinderella, and so much more—lavishly illustrated with original 19th century drawings. 114 illustrations. x + 269pp. 5⅜ × 8½. 21080-4 Pa. $4.95

SUNDIALS, Albert Waugh. Far and away the best, most thorough coverage of ideas, mathematics concerned, types, construction, adjusting anywhere. Over 100 illustrations. 230pp. 5⅜ × 8½. 22947-5 Pa. $5.95

PICTURE HISTORY OF THE NORMANDIE: With 190 Illustrations, Frank O. Braynard. Full story of legendary French ocean liner: Art Deco interiors, design innovations, furnishings, celebrities, maiden voyage, tragic fire, much more. Extensive text. 144pp. 8⅜ × 11¾. 25257-4 Pa. $10.95

THE FIRST AMERICAN COOKBOOK: A Facsimile of "American Cookery," 1796, Amelia Simmons. Facsimile of the first American-written cookbook published in the United States contains authentic recipes for colonial favorites—pumpkin pudding, winter squash pudding, spruce beer, Indian slapjacks, and more. Introductory Essay and Glossary of colonial cooking terms. 80pp. 5⅜ × 8½. 24710-4 Pa. $3.50

101 PUZZLES IN THOUGHT AND LOGIC, C. R. Wylie, Jr. Solve murders and robberies, find out which fishermen are liars, how a blind man could possibly identify a color—purely by your own reasoning! 107pp. 5⅜ × 8½. 20367-0 Pa. $2.50

ANCIENT EGYPTIAN MYTHS AND LEGENDS, Lewis Spence. Examines animism, totemism, fetishism, creation myths, deities, alchemy, art and magic, other topics. Over 50 illustrations. 432pp. 5⅜ × 8½. 26525-0 Pa. $8.95

ANTHROPOLOGY AND MODERN LIFE, Franz Boas. Great anthropologist's classic treatise on race and culture. Introduction by Ruth Bunzel. Only inexpensive paperback edition. 255pp. 5⅜ × 8½. 25245-0 Pa. $6.95

THE TALE OF PETER RABBIT, Beatrix Potter. The inimitable Peter's terrifying adventure in Mr. McGregor's garden, with all 27 wonderful, full-color Potter illustrations. 55pp. 4¼ × 5½. (Available in U.S. only) 22827-4 Pa. $1.75

THREE PROPHETIC SCIENCE FICTION NOVELS, H. G. Wells. *When the Sleeper Wakes, A Story of the Days to Come* and *The Time Machine* (full version). 335pp. 5⅜ × 8½. (Available in U.S. only) 20605-X Pa. $6.95

APICIUS COOKERY AND DINING IN IMPERIAL ROME, edited and translated by Joseph Dommers Vehling. Oldest known cookbook in existence offers readers a clear picture of what foods Romans ate, how they prepared them, etc. 49 illustrations. 301pp. 6⅛ × 9¼. 23563-7 Pa. $7.95

SHAKESPEARE LEXICON AND QUOTATION DICTIONARY, Alexander Schmidt. Full definitions, locations, shades of meaning of every word in plays and poems. More than 50,000 exact quotations. 1,485pp. 6½ × 9¼. 22726-X, 22727-8 Pa., Two-vol. set $31.90

THE WORLD'S GREAT SPEECHES, edited by Lewis Copeland and Lawrence W. Lamm. Vast collection of 278 speeches from Greeks to 1970. Powerful and effective models; unique look at history. 842pp. 5⅜ × 8½. 20468-5 Pa. $12.95

THE BLUE FAIRY BOOK, Andrew Lang. The first, most famous collection, with many familiar tales: Little Red Riding Hood, Aladdin and the Wonderful Lamp, Puss in Boots, Sleeping Beauty, Hansel and Gretel, Rumpelstiltskin; 37 in all. 138 illustrations. 390pp. 5⅜ × 8½.　21437-0 Pa. $6.95

THE STORY OF THE CHAMPIONS OF THE ROUND TABLE, Howard Pyle. Sir Launcelot, Sir Tristram and Sir Percival in spirited adventures of love and triumph retold in Pyle's inimitable style. 50 drawings, 31 full-page. xviii + 329pp. 6½ × 9¼.　21883-X Pa. $7.95

THE MYTHS OF THE NORTH AMERICAN INDIANS, Lewis Spence. Myths and legends of the Algonquins, Iroquois, Pawnees and Sioux with comprehensive historical and ethnological commentary. 36 illustrations. 5⅜ × 8½.

25967-6 Pa. $8.95

GREAT DINOSAUR HUNTERS AND THEIR DISCOVERIES, Edwin H. Colbert. Fascinating, lavishly illustrated chronicle of dinosaur research, 1820's to 1960. Achievements of Cope, Marsh, Brown, Buckland, Mantell, Huxley, many others. 384pp. 5¼ × 8¼.　24701-5 Pa. $7.95

THE TASTEMAKERS, Russell Lynes. Informal, illustrated social history of American taste 1850's–1950's. First popularized categories Highbrow, Lowbrow, Middlebrow. 129 illustrations. New (1979) afterword. 384pp. 6 × 9.

23993-4 Pa. $8.95

DOUBLE CROSS PURPOSES, Ronald A. Knox. A treasure hunt in the Scottish Highlands, an old map, unidentified corpse, surprise discoveries keep reader guessing in this cleverly intricate tale of financial skullduggery. 2 black-and-white maps. 320pp. 5⅜ × 8½. (Available in U.S. only)　25032-6 Pa. $6.95

AUTHENTIC VICTORIAN DECORATION AND ORNAMENTATION IN FULL COLOR: 46 Plates from "Studies in Design," Christopher Dresser. Superb full-color lithographs reproduced from rare original portfolio of a major Victorian designer. 48pp. 9¼ × 12¼.　25083-0 Pa. $7.95

PRIMITIVE ART, Franz Boas. Remains the best text ever prepared on subject, thoroughly discussing Indian, African, Asian, Australian, and, especially, North-ern American primitive art. Over 950 illustrations show ceramics, masks, totem poles, weapons, textiles, paintings, much more. 376pp. 5⅜ × 8.　20025-6 Pa. $7.95

SIDELIGHTS ON RELATIVITY, Albert Einstein. Unabridged republication of two lectures delivered by the great physicist in 1920–21. *Ether and Relativity* and *Geometry and Experience*. Elegant ideas in non-mathematical form, accessible to intelligent layman. vi + 56pp. 5⅜ × 8½.　24511-X Pa. $2.95

THE WIT AND HUMOR OF OSCAR WILDE, edited by Alvin Redman. More than 1,000 ripostes, paradoxes, wisecracks: Work is the curse of the drinking classes, I can resist everything except temptation, etc. 258pp. 5⅜ × 8½.　20602-5 Pa. $4.95

ADVENTURES WITH A MICROSCOPE, Richard Headstrom. 59 adventures with clothing fibers, protozoa, ferns and lichens, roots and leaves, much more. 142 illustrations. 232pp. 5⅜ × 8½.　23471-1 Pa. $3.95

PLANTS OF THE BIBLE, Harold N. Moldenke and Alma L. Moldenke. Standard reference to all 230 plants mentioned in Scriptures. Latin name, biblical reference, uses, modern identity, much more. Unsurpassed encyclopedic resource for scholars, botanists, nature lovers, students of Bible. Bibliography. Indexes. 123 black-and-white illustrations. 384pp. 6 × 9. 25069-5 Pa. $8.95

FAMOUS AMERICAN WOMEN: A Biographical Dictionary from Colonial Times to the Present, Robert McHenry, ed. From Pocahontas to Rosa Parks, 1,035 distinguished American women documented in separate biographical entries. Accurate, up-to-date data, numerous categories, spans 400 years. Indices. 493pp. 6½ × 9¼. 24523-3 Pa. $10.95

THE FABULOUS INTERIORS OF THE GREAT OCEAN LINERS IN HISTORIC PHOTOGRAPHS, William H. Miller, Jr. Some 200 superb photographs capture exquisite interiors of world's great "floating palaces"—1890's to 1980's: *Titanic, Ile de France, Queen Elizabeth, United States, Europa,* more. Approx. 200 black-and-white photographs. Captions. Text. Introduction. 160pp. 8⅜ × 11¾. 24756-2 Pa. $9.95

THE GREAT LUXURY LINERS, 1927–1954: A Photographic Record, William H. Miller, Jr. Nostalgic tribute to heyday of ocean liners. 186 photos of Ile de France, Normandie, Leviathan, Queen Elizabeth, United States, many others. Interior and exterior views. Introduction. Captions. 160pp. 9 × 12. 24056-8 Pa. $10.95

A NATURAL HISTORY OF THE DUCKS, John Charles Phillips. Great landmark of ornithology offers complete detailed coverage of nearly 200 species and subspecies of ducks: gadwall, sheldrake, merganser, pintail, many more. 74 full-color plates, 102 black-and-white. Bibliography. Total of 1,920pp. 8⅜ × 11¼. 25141-1, 25142-X Cloth. Two-vol. set $100.00

THE SEAWEED HANDBOOK: An Illustrated Guide to Seaweeds from North Carolina to Canada, Thomas F. Lee. Concise reference covers 78 species. Scientific and common names, habitat, distribution, more. Finding keys for easy identification. 224pp. 5⅜ × 8½. 25215-9 Pa. $6.95

THE TEN BOOKS OF ARCHITECTURE: The 1755 Leoni Edition, Leon Battista Alberti. Rare classic helped introduce the glories of ancient architecture to the Renaissance. 68 black-and-white plates. 336pp. 8⅜ × 11¼. 25239-6 Pa. $14.95

MISS MACKENZIE, Anthony Trollope. Minor masterpieces by Victorian master unmasks many truths about life in 19th-century England. First inexpensive edition in years. 392pp. 5⅜ × 8½. 25201-9 Pa. $8.95

THE RIME OF THE ANCIENT MARINER, Gustave Doré, Samuel Taylor Coleridge. Dramatic engravings considered by many to be his greatest work. The terrifying space of the open sea, the storms and whirlpools of an unknown ocean, the ice of Antarctica, more—all rendered in a powerful, chilling manner. Full text. 38 plates. 77pp. 9¼ × 12. 22305-1 Pa. $4.95

THE EXPEDITIONS OF ZEBULON MONTGOMERY PIKE, Zebulon Montgomery Pike. Fascinating first-hand accounts (1805–6) of exploration of Mississippi River, Indian wars, capture by Spanish dragoons, much more. 1,088pp. 5⅜ × 8½. 25254-X, 25255-8 Pa. Two-vol. set $25.90

A CONCISE HISTORY OF PHOTOGRAPHY: Third Revised Edition, Helmut Gernsheim. Best one-volume history—camera obscura, photochemistry, daguerreotypes, evolution of cameras, film, more. Also artistic aspects—landscape, portraits, fine art, etc. 281 black-and-white photographs. 26 in color. 176pp. 8⅜ × 11¼. 25128-4 Pa. $13.95

THE DORÉ BIBLE ILLUSTRATIONS, Gustave Doré. 241 detailed plates from the Bible: the Creation scenes, Adam and Eve, Flood, Babylon, battle sequences, life of Jesus, etc. Each plate is accompanied by the verses from the King James version of the Bible. 241pp. 9 × 12. 23004-X Pa. $9.95

WANDERINGS IN WEST AFRICA, Richard F. Burton. Great Victorian scholar/adventurer's invaluable descriptions of African tribal rituals, fetishism, culture, art, much more. Fascinating 19th-century account. 624pp. 5⅜ × 8½. 26890-X Pa. $12.95

FLATLAND, E. A. Abbott. Intriguing and enormously popular science-fiction classic explores the complexities of trying to survive as a two-dimensional being in a three-dimensional world. Amusingly illustrated by the author. 16 illustrations. 103pp. 5⅜ × 8½. 20001-9 Pa. $2.50

THE HISTORY OF THE LEWIS AND CLARK EXPEDITION, Meriwether Lewis and William Clark, edited by Elliott Coues. Classic edition of Lewis and Clark's day-by-day journals that later became the basis for U.S. claims to Oregon and the West. Accurate and invaluable geographical, botanical, biological, meteorological and anthropological material. Total of 1,508pp. 5⅜ × 8½.
21268-8, 21269-6, 21270-X Pa. Three-vol. set $26.85

LANGUAGE, TRUTH AND LOGIC, Alfred J. Ayer. Famous, clear introduction to Vienna, Cambridge schools of Logical Positivism. Role of philosophy, elimination of metaphysics, nature of analysis, etc. 160pp. 5⅜ × 8½. (Available in U.S. and Canada only) 20010-8 Pa. $3.95

MATHEMATICS FOR THE NONMATHEMATICIAN, Morris Kline. Detailed, college-level treatment of mathematics in cultural and historical context, with numerous exercises. For liberal arts students. Preface. Recommended Reading Lists. Tables. Index. Numerous black-and-white figures. xvi + 641pp. 5⅜ × 8½.
24823-2 Pa. $11.95

HANDBOOK OF PICTORIAL SYMBOLS, Rudolph Modley. 3,250 signs and symbols, many systems in full; official or heavy commercial use. Arranged by subject. Most in Pictorial Archive series. 143pp. 8⅛ × 11. 23357-X Pa. $6.95

INCIDENTS OF TRAVEL IN YUCATAN, John L. Stephens. Classic (1843) exploration of jungles of Yucatan, looking for evidences of Maya civilization. Travel adventures, Mexican and Indian culture, etc. Total of 669pp. 5⅜ × 8½.
20926-1, 20927-X Pa., Two-vol. set $11.90

CATALOG OF DOVER BOOKS

DEGAS: An Intimate Portrait, Ambroise Vollard. Charming, anecdotal memoir by famous art dealer of one of the greatest 19th-century French painters. 14 black-and-white illustrations. Introduction by Harold L. Van Doren. 96pp. 5⅜ × 8½.
25131-4 Pa. $4.95

PERSONAL NARRATIVE OF A PILGRIMAGE TO ALMANDINAH AND MECCAH, Richard Burton. Great travel classic by remarkably colorful personality. Burton, disguised as a Moroccan, visited sacred shrines of Islam, narrowly escaping death. 47 illustrations. 959pp. 5⅜ × 8½. 21217-3, 21218-1 Pa., Two-vol. set $19.90

PHRASE AND WORD ORIGINS, A. H. Holt. Entertaining, reliable, modern study of more than 1,200 colorful words, phrases, origins and histories. Much unexpected information. 254pp. 5⅜ × 8½. 20758-7 Pa. $5.95

THE RED THUMB MARK, R. Austin Freeman. In this first Dr. Thorndyke case, the great scientific detective draws fascinating conclusions from the nature of a single fingerprint. Exciting story, authentic science. 320pp. 5⅜ × 8½. (Available in U.S. only) 25210-8 Pa. $6.95

AN EGYPTIAN HIEROGLYPHIC DICTIONARY, E. A. Wallis Budge. Monumental work containing about 25,000 words or terms that occur in texts ranging from 3000 B.C. to 600 A.D. Each entry consists of a transliteration of the word, the word in hieroglyphs, and the meaning in English. 1,314pp. 6⅜ × 10.
23615-3, 23616-1 Pa., Two-vol. set $35.90

THE COMPLEAT STRATEGYST: Being a Primer on the Theory of Games of Strategy, J. D. Williams. Highly entertaining classic describes, with many illustrated examples, how to select best strategies in conflict situations. Prefaces. Appendices. xvi + 268pp. 5⅜ × 8½. 25101-2 Pa. $6.95

THE ROAD TO OZ, L. Frank Baum. Dorothy meets the Shaggy Man, little Button-Bright and the Rainbow's beautiful daughter in this delightful trip to the magical Land of Oz. 272pp. 5⅜ × 8. 25208-6 Pa. $5.95

POINT AND LINE TO PLANE, Wassily Kandinsky. Seminal exposition of role of point, line, other elements in non-objective painting. Essential to understanding 20th-century art. 127 illustrations. 192pp. 6½ × 9¼. 23808-3 Pa. $5.95

LADY ANNA, Anthony Trollope. Moving chronicle of Countess Lovel's bitter struggle to win for herself and daughter Anna their rightful rank and fortune—perhaps at cost of sanity itself. 384pp. 5⅜ × 8½. 24669-8 Pa. $8.95

EGYPTIAN MAGIC, E. A. Wallis Budge. Sums up all that is known about magic in Ancient Egypt: the role of magic in controlling the gods, powerful amulets that warded off evil spirits, scarabs of immortality, use of wax images, formulas and spells, the secret name, much more. 253pp. 5⅜ × 8½. 22681-6 Pa. $4.50

THE DANCE OF SIVA, Ananda Coomaraswamy. Preeminent authority unfolds the vast metaphysic of India: the revelation of her art, conception of the universe, social organization, etc. 27 reproductions of art masterpieces. 192pp. 5⅜ × 8½.
24817-8 Pa. $5.95

CHRISTMAS CUSTOMS AND TRADITIONS, Clement A. Miles. Origin, evolution, significance of religious, secular practices. Caroling, gifts, yule logs, much more. Full, scholarly yet fascinating; non-sectarian. 400pp. 5⅜ × 8½.
23354-5 Pa. $6.95

THE HUMAN FIGURE IN MOTION, Eadweard Muybridge. More than 4,500 stopped-action photos, in action series, showing undraped men, women, children jumping, lying down, throwing, sitting, wrestling, carrying, etc. 390pp. 7⅞ × 10⅝.
20204-6 Cloth. $24.95

THE MAN WHO WAS THURSDAY, Gilbert Keith Chesterton. Witty, fast-paced novel about a club of anarchists in turn-of-the-century London. Brilliant social, religious, philosophical speculations. 128pp. 5⅜ × 8½.
25121-7 Pa. $3.95

A CEZANNE SKETCHBOOK: Figures, Portraits, Landscapes and Still Lifes, Paul Cezanne. Great artist experiments with tonal effects, light, mass, other qualities in over 100 drawings. A revealing view of developing master painter, precursor of Cubism. 102 black-and-white illustrations. 144pp. 8¾ × 6⅜.
24790-2 Pa. $6.95

AN ENCYCLOPEDIA OF BATTLES: Accounts of Over 1,560 Battles from 1479 B.C. to the Present, David Eggenberger. Presents essential details of every major battle in recorded history, from the first battle of Megiddo in 1479 B.C. to Grenada in 1984. List of Battle Maps. New Appendix covering the years 1967–1984. Index. 99 illustrations. 544pp. 6½ × 9¼.
24913-1 Pa. $14.95

AN ETYMOLOGICAL DICTIONARY OF MODERN ENGLISH, Ernest Weekley. Richest, fullest work, by foremost British lexicographer. Detailed word histories. Inexhaustible. Total of 856pp. 6½ × 9¼.
21873-2, 21874-0 Pa., Two-vol. set $19.90

WEBSTER'S AMERICAN MILITARY BIOGRAPHIES, edited by Robert McHenry. Over 1,000 figures who shaped 3 centuries of American military history. Detailed biographies of Nathan Hale, Douglas MacArthur, Mary Hallaren, others. Chronologies of engagements, more. Introduction. Addenda. 1,033 entries in alphabetical order. xi + 548pp. 6½ × 9¼. (Available in U.S. only)
24758-9 Pa. $13.95

LIFE IN ANCIENT EGYPT, Adolf Erman. Detailed older account, with much not in more recent books: domestic life, religion, magic, medicine, commerce, and whatever else needed for complete picture. Many illustrations. 597pp. 5⅜ × 8½.
22632-8 Pa. $8.95

HISTORIC COSTUME IN PICTURES, Braun & Schneider. Over 1,450 costumed figures shown, covering a wide variety of peoples: kings, emperors, nobles, priests, servants, soldiers, scholars, townsfolk, peasants, merchants, courtiers, cavaliers, and more. 256pp. 8⅜ × 11¼.
23150-X Pa. $9.95

THE NOTEBOOKS OF LEONARDO DA VINCI, edited by J. P. Richter. Extracts from manuscripts reveal great genius; on painting, sculpture, anatomy, sciences, geography, etc. Both Italian and English. 186 ms. pages reproduced, plus 500 additional drawings, including studies for *Last Supper, Sforza* monument, etc. 860pp. 7⅞ × 10¾. (Available in U.S. only) 22572-0, 22573-9 Pa., Two-vol. set $31.90

THE ART NOUVEAU STYLE BOOK OF ALPHONSE MUCHA: All 72 Plates from "Documents Decoratifs" in Original Color, Alphonse Mucha. Rare copyright-free design portfolio by high priest of Art Nouveau. Jewelry, wallpaper, stained glass, furniture, figure studies, plant and animal motifs, etc. Only complete one-volume edition. 80pp. 9⅜ × 12¼.   24044-4 Pa. $9.95

ANIMALS: 1,419 COPYRIGHT-FREE ILLUSTRATIONS OF MAMMALS, BIRDS, FISH, INSECTS, ETC., edited by Jim Harter. Clear wood engravings present, in extremely lifelike poses, over 1,000 species of animals. One of the most extensive pictorial sourcebooks of its kind. Captions. Index. 284pp. 9 × 12.
23766-4 Pa. $9.95

OBELISTS FLY HIGH, C. Daly King. Masterpiece of American detective fiction, long out of print, involves murder on a 1935 transcontinental flight—"a very thrilling story"—NY Times. Unabridged and unaltered republication of the edition published by William Collins Sons & Co. Ltd., London, 1935. 288pp. 5⅜ × 8½. (Available in U.S. only)   25036-9 Pa. $5.95

VICTORIAN AND EDWARDIAN FASHION: A Photographic Survey, Alison Gernsheim. First fashion history completely illustrated by contemporary photographs. Full text plus 235 photos, 1840–1914, in which many celebrities appear. 240pp. 6½ × 9¼.   24205-6 Pa. $8.95

THE ART OF THE FRENCH ILLUSTRATED BOOK, 1700–1914, Gordon N. Ray. Over 630 superb book illustrations by Fragonard, Delacroix, Daumier, Doré, Grandville, Manet, Mucha, Steinlen, Toulouse-Lautrec and many others. Preface. Introduction. 633 halftones. Indices of artists, authors & titles, binders and provenances. Appendices. Bibliography. 608pp. 8⅜ × 11¼.   25086-5 Pa. $24.95

THE WONDERFUL WIZARD OF OZ, L. Frank Baum. Facsimile in full color of America's finest children's classic. 143 illustrations by W. W. Denslow. 267pp. 5⅜ × 8½.   20691-2 Pa. $7.95

FOLLOWING THE EQUATOR: A Journey Around the World, Mark Twain. Great writer's 1897 account of circumnavigating the globe by steamship. Ironic humor, keen observations, vivid and fascinating descriptions of exotic places. 197 illustrations. 720pp. 5⅜ × 8½.   26113-1 Pa. $15.95

THE FRIENDLY STARS, Martha Evans Martin & Donald Howard Menzel. Classic text marshalls the stars together in an engaging, non-technical survey, presenting them as sources of beauty in night sky. 23 illustrations. Foreword. 2 star charts. Index. 147pp. 5⅜ × 8½.   21099-5 Pa. $3.95

FADS AND FALLACIES IN THE NAME OF SCIENCE, Martin Gardner. Fair, witty appraisal of cranks, quacks, and quackeries of science and pseudoscience: hollow earth, Velikovsky, orgone energy, Dianetics, flying saucers, Bridey Murphy, food and medical fads, etc. Revised, expanded In the Name of Science. "A very able and even-tempered presentation."—The New Yorker. 363pp. 5⅜ × 8.

20394-8 Pa. $6.95

ANCIENT EGYPT: ITS CULTURE AND HISTORY, J. E Manchip White. From pre-dynastics through Ptolemies: society, history, political structure, religion, daily life, literature, cultural heritage. 48 plates. 217pp. 5⅜ × 8½.   22548-8 Pa. $5.95

SIR HARRY HOTSPUR OF HUMBLETHWAITE, Anthony Trollope. Incisive, unconventional psychological study of a conflict between a wealthy baronet, his idealistic daughter, and their scapegrace cousin. The 1870 novel in its first inexpensive edition in years. 250pp. 5⅜ × 8½. 24953-0 Pa. $6.95

LASERS AND HOLOGRAPHY, Winston E. Kock. Sound introduction to burgeoning field, expanded (1981) for second edition. Wave patterns, coherence, lasers, diffraction, zone plates, properties of holograms, recent advances. 84 illustrations. 160pp. 5⅜ × 8¼. (Except in United Kingdom) 24041-X Pa. $3.95

INTRODUCTION TO ARTIFICIAL INTELLIGENCE: SECOND, EN-LARGED EDITION, Philip C. Jackson, Jr. Comprehensive survey of artificial intelligence—the study of how machines (computers) can be made to act intelli-gently. Includes introductory and advanced material. Extensive notes updating the main text. 132 black-and-white illustrations. 512pp. 5⅜ × 8½. 24864-X Pa. $8.95

HISTORY OF INDIAN AND INDONESIAN ART, Ananda K. Coomaraswamy. Over 400 illustrations illuminate classic study of Indian art from earliest Harappa finds to early 20th century. Provides philosophical, religious and social insights. 304pp. 6⅝ × 9⅜. 25005-9 Pa. $11.95

THE GOLEM, Gustav Meyrink. Most famous supernatural novel in modern European literature, set in Ghetto of Old Prague around 1890. Compelling story of mystical experiences, strange transformations, profound terror. 13 black-and-white illustrations. 224pp. 5⅜ × 8½. (Available in U.S. only) 25025-3 Pa. $6.95

PICTORIAL ENCYCLOPEDIA OF HISTORIC ARCHITECTURAL PLANS, DETAILS AND ELEMENTS: With 1,880 Line Drawings of Arches, Domes, Doorways, Facades, Gables, Windows, etc., John Theodore Haneman. Sourcebook of inspiration for architects, designers, others. Bibliography. Captions. 141pp. 9 × 12. 24605-1 Pa. $7.95

BENCHLEY LOST AND FOUND, Robert Benchley. Finest humor from early 30's, about pet peeves, child psychologists, post office and others. Mostly unavailable elsewhere. 73 illustrations by Peter Arno and others. 183pp. 5⅜ × 8½. 22410-4 Pa. $4.95

ERTÉ GRAPHICS, Erté. Collection of striking color graphics: *Seasons, Alphabet, Numerals, Aces* and *Precious Stones.* 50 plates, including 4 on covers. 48pp. 9⅜ × 12¼. 23580-7 Pa. $7.95

THE JOURNAL OF HENRY D. THOREAU, edited by Bradford Torrey, F. H. Allen. Complete reprinting of 14 volumes, 1837–61, over two million words; the sourcebooks for *Walden,* etc. Definitive. All original sketches, plus 75 photographs. 1,804pp. 8½ × 12¼. 20312-3, 20313-1 Cloth., Two-vol. set $125.00

CASTLES: THEIR CONSTRUCTION AND HISTORY, Sidney Toy. Traces castle development from ancient roots. Nearly 200 photographs and drawings illustrate moats, keeps, baileys, many other features. Caernarvon, Dover Castles, Hadrian's Wall, Tower of London, dozens more. 256pp. 5⅜ × 8¼. 24898-4 Pa. $6.95

CATALOG OF DOVER BOOKS

AMERICAN CLIPPER SHIPS: 1833–1858, Octavius T. Howe & Frederick C. Matthews. Fully-illustrated, encyclopedic review of 352 clipper ships from the period of America's greatest maritime supremacy. Introduction. 109 halftones. 5 black-and-white line illustrations. Index. Total of 928pp. 5⅜ × 8½.
25115-2, 25116-0 Pa., Two-vol. set $17.90

TOWARDS A NEW ARCHITECTURE, Le Corbusier. Pioneering manifesto by great architect, near legendary founder of "International School." Technical and aesthetic theories, views on industry, economics, relation of form to function, "mass-production spirit," much more. Profusely illustrated. Unabridged translation of 13th French edition. Introduction by Frederick Etchells. 320pp. 6⅛ × 9¼. (Available in U.S. only)
25023-7 Pa. $8.95

THE BOOK OF KELLS, edited by Blanche Cirker. Inexpensive collection of 32 full-color, full-page plates from the greatest illuminated manuscript of the Middle Ages, painstakingly reproduced from rare facsimile edition. Publisher's Note. Captions. 32pp. 9⅜ × 12¼.
24345-1 Pa. $4.95

BEST SCIENCE FICTION STORIES OF H. G. WELLS, H. G. Wells. Full novel *The Invisible Man*, plus 17 short stories: "The Crystal Egg," "Aepyornis Island," "The Strange Orchid," etc. 303pp. 5⅜ × 8½. (Available in U.S. only)
21531-8 Pa. $6.95

AMERICAN SAILING SHIPS: Their Plans and History, Charles G. Davis. Photos, construction details of schooners, frigates, clippers, other sailcraft of 18th to early 20th centuries—plus entertaining discourse on design, rigging, nautical lore, much more. 137 black-and-white illustrations. 240pp. 6⅛ × 9¼.
24658-2 Pa. $6.95

ENTERTAINING MATHEMATICAL PUZZLES, Martin Gardner. Selection of author's favorite conundrums involving arithmetic, money, speed, etc., with lively commentary. Complete solutions. 112pp. 5⅜ × 8½.
25211-6 Pa. $2.95

THE WILL TO BELIEVE, HUMAN IMMORTALITY, William James. Two books bound together. Effect of irrational on logical, and arguments for human immortality. 402pp. 5⅜ × 8½.
20291-7 Pa. $7.95

THE HAUNTED MONASTERY and THE CHINESE MAZE MURDERS, Robert Van Gulik. 2 full novels by Van Gulik continue adventures of Judge Dee and his companions. An evil Taoist monastery, seemingly supernatural events; overgrown topiary maze that hides strange crimes. Set in 7th-century China. 27 illustrations. 328pp. 5⅜ × 8½.
23502-5 Pa. $6.95

CELEBRATED CASES OF JUDGE DEE (DEE GOONG AN), translated by Robert Van Gulik. Authentic 18th-century Chinese detective novel; Dee and associates solve three interlocked cases. Led to Van Gulik's own stories with same characters. Extensive introduction. 9 illustrations. 237pp. 5⅜ × 8½.
23337-5 Pa. $5.95

Prices subject to change without notice.
Available at your book dealer or write for free catalog to Dept. GI, Dover Publications, Inc., 31 East 2nd St., Mineola, N.Y. 11501. Dover publishes more than 175 books each year on science, elementary and advanced mathematics, biology, music, art, literary history, social sciences and other areas.